OWN IT! 4

B1 Preliminary test content in Own It! Level 4 has been checked by Cambridge Assessment English for accuracy and level.

STUDENT'S BOOK
WITH DIGITAL PACK

Samantha Lewis and Daniel Vincent
with Andrew Reid

CAMBRIDGE
UNIVERSITY PRESS

CONTENTS

	Vocabulary	Language in action	Reading
Starter Unit Welcome! p4	Travel p4 Music and theatre p4 Ways of communicating p7	Present and past simple and continuous p6 Present perfect and past simple p8	An interview in a school magazine p5
Unit 1 Trendsetters p10	Describing clothes and shoes p11 Verbs related to clothes and shoes p14	Present perfect simple and present perfect continuous p13 Modifiers p15	A blog post: Fashion & technology – Connected clothes p12 A travel guide: Traditional Scottish dress p18 What we wear and why p18
Unit review p20, **Finished?** p118			
Unit 2 Changes p22	Phrasal verbs: changes p23 Parts of objects p26	*used to*, *would* and past simple p25 Past perfect with *never*, *already*, *by (then)*, *by the time* p27	A brochure: ACE Exchanges – discover a new world and a new you! p24 History: Starting again p137
Unit review p32, **Finished?** p119			
Unit 3 Food for thought p34	Cooking verbs p35 Quantities p38	Future tenses p37 Future continuous and future perfect p39	An online forum: class 4C study room p36 An article: A taste of Australia p42 Food in Japan p42
Unit review p44, **Finished?** p120			
Unit 4 Sense and sensitivity p46	The five senses p47 Describing texture, sound, taste, etc. p50	Deduction and possibility p49 Obligation, prohibition, necessity and advice p51	A magazine article: No pain, no fear – No way! p48 Science: Echolocation p138
Unit review p56, **Finished?** p121			

Vocabulary Bank p127–131 CLIL p137–138 Pronunciation p141

Listening	Speaking and pronunciation	Writing	Project	Learn to Learn
A talk p7		An informal email p9		Personalising vocabulary p4 Describing words you don't know with other words or a gesture p7
An interview p14	Giving your opinion politely p16 Everyday English p16 The letters *ea* p141	A blog comment p17		Categorising p11 Recording new verbs p14 Using spidergrams p19 Learn to … write different kinds of example sentences p21
A quiz show p26	Explaining how to use something p28 Everyday English p28 *used to* p141	An opinion essay p29	The history project: a retro museum exhibition p30 *How to* schedule p31	Using words in different situations p23 Identifying key words p26 Learn to … help your partner improve their writing p33
A recipe p38	Giving instructions p40 Everyday English p40 The letters *ch* p141	A listicle p41		Wordbuilding: adjectives from verbs p35 Using diagrams p38 Understanding words from context p43 Learn to … set and achieve learning goals p45
An interview p50	Making guesses and giving clues p52 Everyday English p52 Weak form of *to* p141	An encyclopaedia entry p53	The science project: an infographic on animal senses p54 *How to* research p54	Brainstorming p47 Using visual clues when listening p50 Learn to … plan your homework p57

STARTER

WELCOME!

VOCABULARY

Travel

S.01 **1 Match the words in the box with the photos. Listen, check and repeat.**

accommodation	☐	backpacking	☐
holiday resort	☐	sightseeing	1
tourist attractions	☐	trip	☐

S.02 **2 Complete the comments with the words in Exercise 1. Listen and check.**

Where did you go on holiday this summer?

London. It's a great city for [1] sightseeing because there are so many [2] ________. My favourite was Big Ben.

To a [3] ________ in Greece. The [4] ________ was amazing – a beautiful hotel right next to the beach.

I went [5] ________ in Mexico this summer – just me, my bag, and a paper map. It was the best [6] ________ of my life.

LEARN TO LEARN

Personalising vocabulary

Writing sentences helps you to remember words.

Use it!

3 Write true sentences about your holidays with the words in Exercise 1.

____

____

____

Music and theatre

S.03 **4 Match the nouns in the box with the definitions. Listen, check and repeat.**

audience lines part ~~rehearsal~~ scene show

1. When people practise a play rehearsal
2. live performance in a theatre ________
3. the words actors say ________
4. a character in a play ________
5. the people who watch ________
6. a part of a play ________

Use it!

5 Complete the questions with words in Exercise 4. Discuss the questions.

1. Have you ever been in a show at school? What ________ did you play? How did you learn your ________? Did you have any ________ before the show?
2. How is the ________ at the theatre and cinema different to at a concert?
3. If you were in a film, would you like to appear all the way through the film, or be in one big, important ________?

Explore it!

Guess the correct answer.

What films do these lines come from?

a 'To infinity and beyond!'

b 'Just keep swimming.'

Write other famous lines from English films. Can your partner guess the film?

READING

An interview in a school magazine

S.04 **1** **Look at the photo. What do you think the boy is doing? Read the interview and check your answer.**

Now that we're back to school, everybody's talking about what they did in the summer. Some of you probably stayed in a holiday resort or went sightseeing with your family, and most of you probably spent time at the pool with friends. But not Joshua Wills. His summer was very different. Let's find out why.

Joshua, you didn't have a normal summer holiday this year, did you? What did you do?

No, I didn't. I took part in a theatre camp for teenagers. Our teachers were real actors from the theatre and TV. They taught us all about acting – you know, how to develop a character, how to project your voice and use your body. It was lots of fun.

Did you put on a show?

We put on a musical about a detective. I played the part of the detective's assistant. We had one rehearsal every day for a week, and then three performances. Lots of my friends and family came.

How did it go?

It was great, but on the first night, in the final scene, I forgot my lines. Everything was going really well and then suddenly I couldn't remember anything! Everyone in the audience was looking at me, thinking, 'What's wrong? He's not speaking. He's not even moving!'

Were you panicking?

I wasn't panicking. I was just frozen! But in the end I remembered the lines and it was all OK.

Do you want to do more theatre?

Definitely! I don't want to stop. In fact, I'm writing a play. It's more difficult than I expected, but I'm really enjoying it. I want to put it on at school.

Are you looking for any actors?

Of course! Why? Do you want to join us?

Maybe! It sounds like fun!

2 **Read the interview again and answer the questions.**

1 Why was Joshua's summer holiday unusual?

______

2 What did the theatre camp participants learn?

______

3 How often did the group practise their play?

______

4 What problem did Joshua have?

______

5 How did the audience react to the problem?

______

6 Why is Joshua looking for actors now?

______

3 **Find words in the interview that mean:**

1 speak loudly and clearly (phrase) ______
2 somebody who helps someone do their job (n) ______
3 unable to move (adj) ______
4 100% yes! (adv) ______

Voice it!

4 **Discuss the questions.**

1 Joshua's teachers were real actors. What is good about this?
2 Have you ever acted or spoken in front of a big group of people? How was it?

LANGUAGE IN ACTION

Present and past simple and continuous

Watch video S.1
What did he do every day?
What's he doing now?

Present simple	Present continuous	Past simple	Past continuous
It **sounds** like fun.	I [1]_____ **writing** a play.	We **had** one rehearsal every day.	Everybody in the audience [2]_____ **looking** at me.
I [3]_____ **want** to stop.	He **isn't speaking**.	You [4]_____ **have** a normal summer holiday this year.	I [5]_____ **panicking**.
[6]_____ you **want** to try?	[7]_____ you **looking** for actors?	What [8]_____ you **do**?	**Were** you **panicking**?

1 **Complete the examples in the table above with the correct form of *be* or *do*. Use the interview on page 5 to help you.**

S.05 **2** **Complete the sentences with the correct form of the verbs in brackets. Listen and check.**

1 Mike ___*goes*___ (go) sightseeing every year.
2 Amalia __________ (not learn) her lines until the night before the first show.
3 A Where's Harry? B He __________ (read) in his room.
4 You didn't like the play, did you, Emir? You __________ (sleep) during it!
5 I'm so happy we __________ (not stay) in that holiday resort last week when the terrible storm came.
6 Ana's not at the rehearsal because she __________ (not feel) well right now.

3 **Complete Esma's blog with the correct form of the verbs in the box.**

begin do get up go ~~have~~ not finish
not forget practise start think

Hi, everyone. Yesterday we [1]*had* our last rehearsal for the musical. I [2]_____ practising until 11 pm, and when I [3]_____ to bed, some of the others [4]_____ still _____. The first show [5]_____ at 7.30 tonight. I didn't feel nervous when I [6]_____ this morning, but I [7]_____ to feel nervous now – I hope I [8]_____ my lines. But I'm also really excited. I [9]_____ it's going to be a great night. Anyway, [10]_____ you _____ anything this weekend? Why don't you come and see me?

Use it!

4 **Write the questions.**

1 what / you / do / at nine o'clock last night
What were you doing at nine o'clock last night?
2 what time / you / get up / today
____
3 during the summer / you / prefer to go sightseeing or go to the beach
____
4 what time / you / usually / get up / when you're on holiday
____
5 speak English to anyone / last week
____
6 what / you / wear / at the moment
____

5 **Ask and answer the questions.**

What were you doing at nine o'clock last night?

I was watching some videos online.

VOCABULARY AND LISTENING

Ways of communicating

S.06 **1** **Match the verbs in the box with the emoticons 1–9. Listen, check and repeat.**

describe	☐	greet	☐	post	☐
shake hands	1	shout	☐	smile	☐
translate	☐	wave	☐	whisper	☐

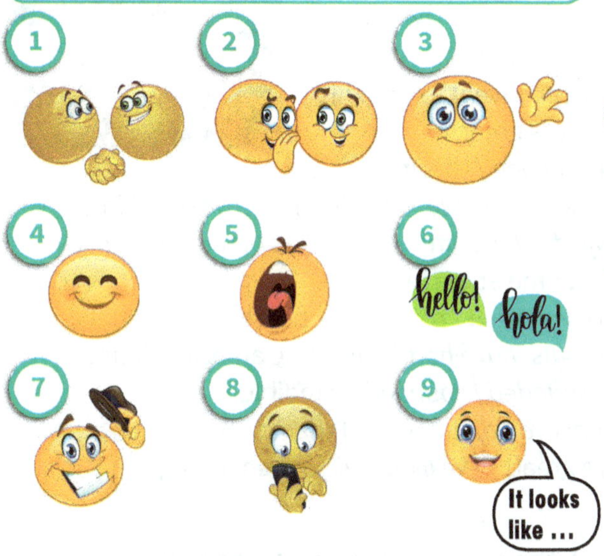

S.07 **2** **Listen to the dialogues and circle the correct words in Exercise 1.**

1 whisper / shake hands
2 translate / smile
3 post / shout
4 greet / translate
5 wave / describe

3 **Do we express the verbs in Exercise 1 with actions or words? Complete the table.**

Actions	Words
shake hands	describe

LEARN TO LEARN

Describing words you don't know with other words or a gesture

When you don't know a word, use words you do know to describe it or use gestures to express what you mean.

4 **Express or explain the words in the box with other words or gestures.**

accommodation cry dance film frozen sing stand up tourist attraction

It's a place where you can stay. *Accommodation?*

Use it!

5 **Use gestures or tell your partner *I do this when ….* Can they guess the verb?**

A talk

S.08 **6** **Listen to Mateo and tick (✓) the tips that helped him learn English.**

a Describe a word with other words ☐
b Do a language course ☐
c Don't worry about making mistakes ☐
d Listen to music ☐
e Talk as much as possible ☐
f Translate words and make them sound English ☐
g Watch TV ☐

S.08 **7** **Listen again and complete each sentence with one word.**

1 Mateo is studying ________ at university.
2 He didn't understand the family at first because they ________ so fast.
3 When he doesn't know a word, he describes it, ________ it or makes a word in English similar to the Spanish word.
4 Lots of things were different for him, but he liked the ________ best.

Voice it!

8 **Discuss the questions.**

1 Which of Mateo's tips do you use?
2 Which tips would you like to try?

Watch video S.2
Where did she go last summer?
Which language has she never studied?

LANGUAGE IN ACTION

Present perfect and past simple

Present perfect	Past simple
I've been at university now for three months.	I **started** my course in October.
I **haven't stopped** [1]_____ I was there! I**'ve** [2]_____ **been** to London.	I **met** lots of people in the first few weeks.
Have you [3]_____ **been** to London?	**Did** you **go** to London last year?

1 **Complete the examples in the table above with *ever*, *since* or *never*.**

Get it right!

We don't use the present simple with *since*.

*We've **been** here **since** Tuesday.*

NOT ~~We are here since Tuesday.~~

2 **Look at sentences a–d. Circle the correct options to complete the rules.**

a Last year I **spent** six months in London.

b I **didn't understand** the kids because they **spoke** fast.

c I**'ve watched** every episode of *The Big Bang Theory*.

d I**'ve stayed** in contact with people I **met** in London.

1 Use the *present perfect / past simple* for things that happened in a finished time period, e.g. last year.

2 Use the *present perfect / past simple* for things that happened in the past in an unfinished time period, or when the exact time of the action is not important.

S.09 **3** **Circle the correct words. Listen and check.**

BEN [1]*Have you ever been* / *Did you ever go* to a music festival?

JESSIE Yeah, [2]*I've been* / *went* to one this summer. It was great.

BEN Where [3]*has it been* / *was it*?

JESSIE Near the town where we [4]*have been* / *went* on holiday. [5]*We've stayed* / *stayed* in the town lots of times but this was our first time at the festival.

BEN What [6]*have you liked* / *did you like* best?

JESSIE The Night Owls [7]*have had* / *had* some amazing dancers and [8]*have sounded* / *sounded* incredible.

BEN [9]*I've never heard* / *didn't hear* of them.

JESSIE Oh, they're great! [10]*I've liked* / *liked* them for ages.

4 **Complete the text with the past simple or present perfect.**

I [1] _have_ never _been_ (be) to Mexico, but last summer I [2]__________ (get) a job in a Mexican restaurant. I [3]__________ (meet) loads of people since I [4]__________ (start) working there and I [5]__________ (make) friends. At first they [6]__________ (speak) to me in Spanish, but I [7]__________ (not understand). Since then I [8]__________ (go) to Spanish classes and I [9]__________ (learn) lots. Our teacher [10]__________ (teach) us how to describe things when we don't know the exact word.

Use it!

5 **Discuss the questions.**

1 How many cities in your country have you visited?

2 How long have you know your best friend?

3 Have you ever been to a festival?

I've been to three cities. I went to the capital last month, but there are some cities I've never been to.

WRITING
An informal email

1 **Look at the photos. What can you see? Read Azra's email and put the photos in the correct order.**

a 
b 
c 

2 **Read the email again. Why did Azra write the email? What did she enjoy about her visit?**

[1]From:	azra.kara@myemail.com
[2]To:	gaby.bates@myemail.com
[3]Subject:	Thank you

[4]Hi Gaby,

[5]How are things? [6]I just wanted to say thank you for a great visit to Manchester. I had an amazing time and your family are so kind!

I loved meeting your friends and visiting the city. There's so much to see! I learned so much about the UK that I didn't know before. I've listened to the playlist you made me lots of times since I got back home and I know all the words to the songs!

I've told my friends all about my trip and they're really looking forward to meeting you next month. I can't wait to take you sightseeing in Istanbul to show you all the tourist attractions and introduce you to my friends and family. We've bought tickets to go and watch a Turkish dance show while you're here – I hope you like it!

[7]Write back soon,

[8]Love Azra

3 **Match the letters a–h with the parts of the email 1–8.**

a Address of the recipient ☐
b Address of the sender 1
c Ending and your name ☐
d First sentence ☐
e Last sentence ☐
f Reason you are writing ☐
g Beginning and name ☐
h Topic of the email ☐

4 **Complete the *Useful language* box with phrases from the email.**

Useful language

Starting and ending an informal email

Start + name: Hello Gaby / [1] ____________

First sentence: How are you? / Thanks for your email / [2] ____________ ?

The reason you are writing: I'm writing to / [3] ____________

Last sentence: See you soon. / Bye for now. / [4] ____________

End + name: Take care, Azra / [5] ____________

Write your own informal email to a friend.

PLAN

5 **Imagine you are doing an exchange with someone in an English-speaking country. You have visited their country and they are going to visit yours. Make notes about these things.**

where you went ____________________

what you did ____________________

what you liked about your visit ____________________

what you are going to do when they visit you ____________________

WRITE

6 **Write your email. Remember to include language and vocabulary from this unit, phrases from the *Useful language* box, the parts of the email in Exercise 3 and the ideas in Exercise 5.**

CHECK

7 **Do you …**

- start and end the email correctly?
- give the reason why you are writing?
- say what you are going to do when your friend visits?

1 TRENDSETTERS

LEARNING OUTCOMES

I can ...

- understand texts about technology and fashion
- give my opinion politely
- comment on a blog post
- understand how to use the present perfect simple and continuous and modifiers
- talk about and describe clothes and shoes
- categorise adjectives, record new verbs, use spidergrams for associated words.

Start it!

1 Look at the photo. Do you like the clothes that the people are wearing? Why? / Why not?
2 Before you watch, what does fashion mean to you?
3 Name three ways fashion changed in the 1960s. Watch and check.
4 What is your favourite fashion style?

Watch video 1.1

p13

Language in action 1.2

p15

Language in action 1.3

p16

Everyday English 1.4

p18

Globetrotters 1.5

VOCABULARY
Describing clothes and shoes

1.01 **1** **Match the adjectives in bold with the numbers in the photos. Listen, check and repeat.**

baggy trousers	☐	**checked** shirt	☐
denim skirt	☐	**flat** shoes	☐
flowery dress	☐	**high-heeled** boots	☐
long-sleeved dress	☐	**plain cotton** T-shirt	☐
spotted shoes	☐	**striped** T-shirt	☐
tight jeans	1		

1.02 **2** **Juan and Rosa are shopping for clothes for a school party. Listen to the conversation. Which things in Exercise 1 do they buy?**

____

____

LEARN TO LEARN
Categorising

When we use lots of adjectives to describe one thing, we use this order: shape, colour, pattern, material.

3 **Complete the table with the adjectives in Exercise 1.**

Shape	Pattern	Material

4 **Write three sentences describing the clothes in Exercise 1. Use at least two adjectives in each sentence.**

She's wearing a white cotton T-shirt.

1 ______________________________

2 ______________________________

3 ______________________________

5 **Read your sentences in Exercise 4. Can your partner guess which photo you are describing?**

Use it!

6 **Discuss the questions.**

1 Which clothes in Exercise 1 do you have?
2 Can you describe the clothes you are wearing?
3 Which shapes, patterns and materials do you usually wear? Which do you never wear?

Explore it!

Guess the correct answer.

Some celebrities wear special 'anti-paparazzi' scarves. What do you think these scarves do?

a make their faces more beautiful
b make the photos go black
c make the celebrities look ugly

Find out about a clothes designer. Write a question for your partner to answer.

Fashion & technology

CONNECTED CLOTHES

Anyone who has been reading my blog for a while knows that I'm a huge fan of technology in fashion. Here are my latest discoveries.

A We've all seen watches that measure how much we move or sleep, but what about a T-shirt? Over the last few years, scientists have been developing clothes which can record information about our heart rate or breathing and which can help us stay healthy. Most people have a denim jacket. But have you ever seen a denim jacket that can play music or send instant messages? Well, scientists have designed one that can. You just have to touch the sleeve and your music starts playing!

B Scientists have also created clothes with sensors that take our body temperature and circulate warm or cool air through the material so that we never feel too hot or too cold. Special clothes for astronauts or emergency service workers have been using this technology for years, but now companies have created similar materials for everyday clothing and shoes. Great! No more hot, sweaty feet!

C Now there are even smart clothes that produce energy while we're wearing them! Scientists in South Korea have created a material that turns movement into electricity. So, you can charge your phone while you're doing exercise or just walking around! That's smart!

D Finally, if you haven't been following my updates on 3-D printing, check out these trendy designs. My favourite is the high-heeled shoes. I love the fact that each design is individual and that one day we'll be able to design and print our own patterned or plain clothes and shoes at home.

READING

A blog post

1 Look at the pictures. How do they combine technology and fashion?

2 Read the blog post. Match headings 1–4 with paragraphs A–D. 1.03

1 3-D printed clothes _____
2 Clothes that change temperature _____
3 Connected clothing _____
4 Energy-producing clothes _____

3 Read the blog post again and answer the questions.

1 How can we watch our health with connected clothing?
____
2 How does the denim jacket in the text play music?
____
3 What's good about creating electricity with clothes?
____
4 What does the blogger predict about 3-D printed clothes?
____

4 Find words in the blog that mean:

1 the part of clothing that covers your arm (A) ______
2 to move around something (B) ______
3 to put electricity into a device like a phone (C) ______
4 the latest information (D) ______
5 to produce something with a printer (D) ______

Voice it!

5 Discuss the questions.

1 Would you like to have any of the smart clothes in the blog?
2 What other things would you like clothes to do in the future?
3 Do you think smart clothes are important? Why / Why not?

Finished? p118 Ex 1

Watch video 1.2
How long has Tara been knitting?
How many people have bought Patrick's shoes?

LANGUAGE IN ACTION

Present perfect simple and present perfect continuous

Present perfect simple	Present perfect continuous
Scientists [1]______ also **created** clothes with sensors.	Over the last few years, scientists [2]______ **been developing** clothes which can record information.
He [3]______ **bought** any 3-D printed clothing yet.	If you [4]______ **been following** my updates on 3-D printing, check out these trendy designs.
[5]______ you ever **seen** a jacket that can play music?	How long [6]______ you **been reading** my blog?

1 **Complete the examples in the table above with the correct form of *have*.**

2 **Complete the rules with *simple* or *continuous*.**

1 In present perfect ______ sentences the focus is on the result of an activity.
2 In present perfect ______ sentences the focus is on how long the activity is.

3 **Put the words in the correct order to make sentences.**

1 lots of / I've / blog posts / written
   I've written lots of blog posts.
2 since / a fashion blog / writing / She's been / January
   ____
3 made / Have you / your own clothes / ever / ?
   ____
4 been / He's / two years / designing / for / clothes
   ____

1.04 **4** **Complete the text with the present perfect continuous form of the verbs in the box. Listen and check.**

help	make	not practise	~~try~~	watch	work

Recently I [1] 've been trying to learn how to knit. It's really difficult! I [2]______ lots of videos online, but I [3]______ very much. I [4]______ a scarf for a few days now, but it's full of holes and looks awful. My mum [5]______ me too, but she [6]______ all week and hasn't really got much free time.

1.05 **5** **Complete the sentences with the present perfect simple or continous form of the verbs in brackets. Listen, check and repeat.**

1 How long has he been designing clothes? (design)
2 ______ you ever ______ to knit? (learn)
3 She ______ never ______ high-heeled shoes. (wear)
4 I ______ in these shoes all morning and my feet really hurt! (walk).

Use it!

6 **Imagine you are a fashion designer. Make questions with the present perfect simple or continuous. Then think of your answers.**

1 What / designed?
   ____
2 Who / worn your designs?
   ____
3 How long / designing clothes?
   ____

7 **Ask and answer the questions. Which designer makes the most interesting clothes? Why?**

I've designed a coat which changes colour when it gets wet!

Finished? p118 Ex 2

VOCABULARY AND LISTENING

Verbs related to clothes and shoes

1.06 **1 Read the fashion forum and match the verbs in bold with the definitions. Listen, check and repeat.**

ARE YOU A FOLLOWER OF FASHION?

MARIA I don't buy many clothes because they **go out of fashion** so quickly. I usually buy things that **go with** other clothes I already have. I like wearing green clothes because they **match** my eyes!

GISELA I'm really tall so it's difficult to find clothes that **fit** me, especially jeans! I wear jeans so much they **wear out**! Lots of clothes don't **suit** me, because they haven't been designed for tall people.

EDU I love fashion and I work in a clothes store on Saturdays. It's great because I get to try on loads of clothes. The worst part is the changing rooms. People leave clothes on the floor and I have to **hang up** the jackets and trousers and **fold** all the T-shirts. It takes forever!

IRINA Today I had a complete fashion disaster. I was trying on a dress in a shop. I managed to **do up** the zip! But when I tried to take the dress off I couldn't **undo** it. How embarrassing!

1. be the right size _fit_
2. not popular any longer ______
3. wear something so much it looks old ______
4. make someone look good ______
5. look good together ______
6. be similar or the same colour/type ______
7. close buttons or zips on clothes ______
8. open buttons or zips on clothes ______
9. put clothes on a coat hanger ______
10. bend clothes so that one part lies on another part ______

LEARN TO LEARN

Recording new verbs

Make sentences with new verbs so that you can remember how to use them.

2 Complete the sentences with the correct form of the verbs in the box and the words in brackets.

do up	hang up	not go with	suit	~~wear out~~

1. You never _wear out your shoes_. They always look new. (your shoes)
2. That colour ______. It looks good. (you)
3. This top ______. They're different styles. (my skirt)
4. ______ on your jacket. It's cold. (the zip)

Get it right!

The word *clothes* is always plural.

Your new clothes look great!

Use it!

3 Discuss the questions.

1. Which clothes fit you well?
2. Which ones suit you?
3. Which ones have you worn out?

An interview

1.07 **4 Listen to an interview with Carla. Where does she get her clothes from?**

1.07 **5 Listen again and complete the text.**

Carla started looking at fashion designs online when she was [1] _12_. She enjoys upcycling – creating [2] ______ from something that exists. She also decorates [3] ______ T-shirts and tops with her own designs. She knows that people buy fast fashion because the clothes are [4] ______ and that ethical fashion is [5] ______ than fast fashion but ethical fashion thinks about the people who [6] ______.

Pronunciation p141

LANGUAGE IN ACTION
Modifiers

Watch video 1.3
What are the top three fashion mistakes? What's the problem if your bedroom is totally messy?

I've been [1]______ obsessed with fashion since I was a child.	**a** extremely / absolutely / ______ / really
They look [2]______ good.	**b** quite / rather / fairly / ______
These clothes are [3]______ more expensive …	**c** ______ / a little
but they last [4]______ longer.	**d** ______ / far

1 Complete the examples in the table above with *a bit*, *a lot*, *pretty* and *totally*. Use the same words in each line.

2 Which words (a–d) do we use before …

1 comparative adjectives to show a big difference? ______
2 comparative adjectives to show a small difference? ______
3 strong adjectives? ______
4 adjectives to mean more than *a little* but less than *very*? ______

1.10 **3 Circle the correct words. Listen and check.**

Making materials like cotton or denim can be [1]*extremely / a lot* damaging for the environment. That's why it's [2]*absolutely / far* essential we create new materials from natural products that are [3]*fairly / a lot* better for the planet. Some materials like bamboo have been [4]*fairly / a little* successful. Others are still being developed, like a material from the rice plant, which is [5]*quite / a bit* similar to cotton, and one made from chicken feathers, which is [6]*pretty / a bit* warm, like wool. Technology has also made it [7]*really / far* easier to recycle materials like plastic bottles into clothes such as leggings and T-shirts, which is [8]*really / a lot* good news for the environment!

4 Complete the sentences with the words in brackets.

1 I feel __quite__ tired today. I need to sleep well otherwise I'll be __extremely__ tired tomorrow. (extremely / quite)
2 The shopping centre in our town is ______ good, but the one outside town is ______ better. (far / quite)
3 He creates ______ amazing designs, which are ______ more fun than ours. (a lot / totally)
4 I'm ______ good at art, but there are people in my class who are ______ more talented than me. (far / fairly)
5 This coat is ______ beautiful and it's only ______ more expensive than the other one. (a bit / absolutely)

Use it!

5 Complete the sentences so they are true for you.

1 I am pretty good at ______.
2 I feel quite sad when ______.
3 A subject I find a lot easier than before is ______.
4 I'm a bit more interested in ______ than before.
5 I think it's absolutely amazing that ______.

6 Guess what your partner wrote in their sentences. Score one point for each correct guess.

Did you say, 'I am pretty good at English'?

No, I didn't. I said, 'I'm pretty good at art'.

Finished? p118 Ex 3

SPEAKING
Giving your opinion politely

1.11 **1 Listen to the conversation. Does Diego like the things?**

DIEGO Hey, Dana. How's it going?
DANA Hi Diego. I've been shopping all morning. I've bought some great stuff. Do you want to see?
DIEGO Yeah, sure.
DANA I got this striped jacket from Zaps, that new store they've just opened.
DIEGO Oh right. Wow! ¹ That's … er … different!
DANA I know! It's totally out there!
DIEGO Mmm, ² ________________ yellow and blue together, but the blue matches the colour of your eyes.
DANA Thanks! And check out these trousers.
DIEGO Flowery trousers! Wow! Very retro!
DANA I know! They fit really well. What do you think?
DIEGO Well, ³ ________________, but I can see why you like them.
DANA Do you think they suit me?
DIEGO Yes, I guess so.
DANA I think I might wear them to go out later, with the jacket.
DIEGO Mmm, ⁴ ________________ I'd wear them together. ⁵ ________________ the trousers would go better with a plain top.
DANA No, patterns are totally in this year.
DIEGO You're such a fashion victim, Dana!

1.11 **2 Complete the conversation with the phrases from the *Useful language* box. Listen and check.**

Useful language

I don't know if … I'm not a huge fan of …
I think maybe … That's … er … different!
They're not exactly my style.

Watch video 1.4
Everyday English

check out fashion victim in out there

3 Match the phrases in the *Everyday English* box with the words and phrases 1–4.

1 someone who follows fashion ____________
2 fashionable ____________
3 different ____________
4 look at ____________

PLAN

4 Write about the clothes in the photo:

What clothes are they?
Who bought them and why?
What do they look like?
Why do you like or not like them?

SPEAK

5 Practise the conversation with your partner. Remember to use the present perfect simple and continuous, modifiers, the vocabulary from this unit and phrases from the *Useful language* and *Everyday English* boxes.

CHECK

6 Work with another pair. Listen to their conversation and complete the notes.

Who bought them and why? ____________
____
What do they look like? ____________
____
Do the other pair like them? ____________
____

Four steps
to reduce your fashion footprint

Here are some ideas you can try!

- Have a clothes swap party. Swap clothes you don't want with your friends.
- Save energy. Wash clothes less often, dry clothes naturally, don't iron!
- Give old clothes to second-hand shops. Don't throw them away!
- Buy fewer, better quality new clothes.

Comments

Great post! It got me thinking about how to reduce my fashion footprint. I talked to my parents and we decided to try and reduce the amount of energy we use on our clothes. Usually we wash all our clothes every time we wear them, even when they're still pretty clean, but this month we've been washing clothes less often, and we haven't ironed anything. My parents have saved money and I've been much better at hanging up my clothes! Carlos

Thanks for sharing! I had no idea that I throw so many clothes away! I had a clothes swap party last week. I got a great denim jacket that I absolutely love! I also got two long-sleeved tops and some cool high-heeled boots for free! I was absolutely amazed that we swapped everything! Since reading your post I've decided to buy far fewer new clothes in the future. Amie

WRITING
A blog comment

1 **Look at the blog post. How can people reduce their fashion footprint?**

2 **Read the blog comments. Answer the questions.**

1 Were the ideas that Carlos and Amie tried successful? How do you know?

____

2 What does Amie want to do in the future?

____

3 **Find the phrases from the *Useful language* box in the blog comments. Which phrases can you use when you …**

1 enjoy reading a post?

____

2 learn something new from the post?

____

3 change your behaviour because of the post?

____

Useful language

Great post!	We decided to …
I had no idea that …	Since reading your post I've …
It got me thinking about …	Thanks for sharing!

Write your own blog comment.

PLAN

4 **Look at the ideas in the blog post and make notes about which one to write about.**

Which ideas will you try out? ______________________

Do you think it will go well? Why? / Why not?

____

What other ideas would you like to try in the future? ______________________

WRITE

5 **Write your blog comment. Remember to include the present perfect simple and continuous, modifiers, vocabulary from this unit and phrases from the *Useful language* box.**

CHECK

6 **Do you …**

- explain why an idea might or might not work well?
- explain what you would like to try in the future?

Finished? p118 Ex 4

AROUND THE WORLD

READING
A travel guide

1.12 **1 Are the sentences about the kilt true or false? Read the travel guide and check your answers.**

1. Kilts are only worn by men. ________
2. Kilts have not always been made of tartan. ________
3. Tartans today indicate where people live. ________
4. Scottish dress is different for men and women. ________
5. Tartan patterns are popular outside Scotland. ________

Globetrotters
Watch video 1.5
What we wear and why

- Why do we wear clothes and what do they show about us?
- What is a *deel* and why do Mongolian people wear it?
- What do the colours blue, white, green, yellow and orange represent for the Masai people?

Traditional Scottish dress

You have probably seen photos of Scotland's most famous piece of clothing, the kilt. But did you know that Scottish men have been wearing kilts for centuries? A kilt used to be an extremely long piece of heavy plain or checked material that men from the Scottish Highlands wore every day. They wrapped the material around their waist and over one shoulder or their head to protect them from the cold wind or rain. Nowadays, the design of the kilt is totally different. It is knee-length and made from wool, with a pattern of vertical and horizontal stripes in different colours called tartan. Tartan designs used to indicate the area where people lived and were far less colourful than they are today. Since the 18th century, people have been wearing tartan designs that represent their family name or clan (group of families) and today there are over 4,500 designs! The kilt forms part of the traditional Highland dress, which is quite different for men and women.

MEN:
- tartan kilt and a kilt pin
- leather belt
- sporran – a small leather or fur bag that hangs from the belt. There are no pockets in a kilt!
- plain or tartan socks
- kilt knife – a small knife kept in one sock
- ghillies – plain, flat leather shoes with long laces

WOMEN:
- long or knee-length tartan kilt
- tartan shawl – a piece of material worn over your shoulders
- plain or tartan socks
- ghillies

2 Use the travel guide to complete the table.

Kilts in the 18th century	Kilts in the 21st century
One long piece of cloth worn around waist and over shoulder	
Highland dress for men	**Highland dress for women**
Who wears traditional tartan clothes?	**Who wears modern tartan clothes?**

Highland dress is extremely popular in Scotland for special occasions such as weddings, funerals or parties, particularly for men. Women often wear kilts to do traditional Scottish dancing at sports and cultural events. Nowadays, tartan isn't just used for traditional dress in Scotland. Fashion designers around the world use tartan to create modern designs such as tartan trousers or tartan shoes and celebrities from Rihanna to Shawn Mendes have been photographed wearing tartan. Even though people have worn tartan for centuries, it is still popular today and looks like it's not going to go out of fashion any time soon.

3 Find the nouns and match them with the definitions.

dress funeral laces pin shawl

1 a ceremony when a person dies ______
2 a combination of clothes worn together for a particular situation ______
3 a small piece of metal to attach clothes ______
4 a large piece of cloth worn over your shoulders or head ______
5 string used to fasten shoes ______

LEARN TO LEARN

Using spidergrams

Spidergrams can help you remember words that have a link with other words.

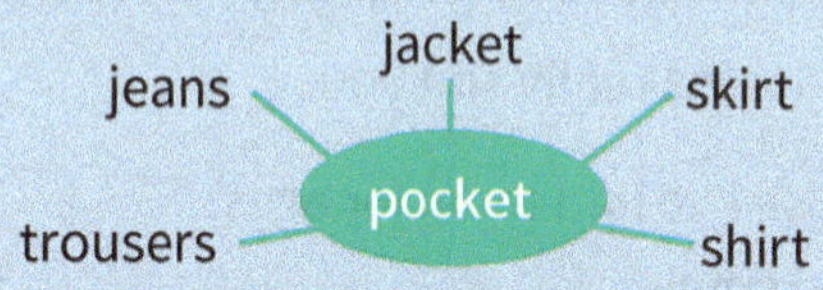

4 Make a spidergram of clothes and shoes which have laces, a zip, buttons or sleeves.

5 Which words did you both write? Add any new words to your spidergrams.

Voice it!

6 Discuss the questions.

1 What is traditional dress in your country?
2 When do people wear it?

Explore it!

Guess the correct answer.

It was illegal to wear tartan in the middle of the 18th century in Scotland. True or false?

a true b false

Find another fact about traditional Scottish dress. Write a question for your partner to answer.

OWN IT! The Culture Project Teacher's Resource Bank

1 REVIEW

VOCABULARY

1 Circle the odd word out.

1	baggy	tight	spotted
2	cotton	long-sleeved	denim
3	flowery	flat	plain
4	cotton	striped	checked
5	plain	flat	high-heeled

2 Match 1–5 with a–e.

1 **Hang up** your clothes, ☐
2 I can't **undo** my jacket, ☐
3 These jeans are **worn out** ☐
4 This T-shirt **doesn't fit** me any more, ☐
5 Your glasses really **suit** you, ☐

a because I've had them for ages.
b it's too small.
c the zip's broken.
d they look great!
e they're all over the floor.

LANGUAGE IN ACTION

3 Complete the text with the present perfect simple or continuous form of the verbs in brackets.

16-year-old Moziah Bridges [1]__________ (design) ties since he was nine. His grandmother taught him to make bow ties and since then he [2]__________ (own) his own business. The designer [3]__________ (appear) in magazines and on TV and [4]__________ (make) a collection of ties for basketball teams in the USA. Mo is still at school but [5]__________ (work) in the evenings. It [6]__________ (not be) easy, but his mum helps him and he [7]__________ (employ) more people as his business [8]__________ (grow). Mo often gives talks to other people who [9]__________ (think) about starting a business.

4 Circle the correct modifier to complete the sentences.

1 It takes *a little / quite* longer to fold your clothes, but then you don't have to iron them.
2 Where did you get that jacket? I *far / absolutely* love it!
3 The second film in the series was *a bit / pretty* better than the first one, but not much.
4 I speak *a lot / fairly* good Chinese, but I can't write it.
5 I'm *far / totally* confused by his explanation. I don't understand it at all.
6 Have you seen this video? It's *really / a lot* funny.
7 That T-shirt is *far / really* nicer than the other one, but it's *quite / a lot* expensive.

Self-assessment

- I can use words to describe clothes and shoes.
- I can use verbs to talk about clothes and shoes.
- I can use the *present perfect simple* and *present perfect continuous*.
- I can use modifiers.

LEARN TO LEARN

LEARN TO … WRITE DIFFERENT KINDS OF EXAMPLE SENTENCES

You can write different kinds of example sentences to help you understand and remember new words.

1 **Read Ela's blog. Why does she recommend using the different kinds of example sentences to remember new words?**

Ela's English learning BLOG

Today's tip: example sentences

Hi everyone! Today we're looking at a great way to learn vocabulary: example sentences. When I learn new words, I often use them in sentences to help me learn and remember them. There are different types of example sentences you can use. They're all good for different reasons.

a sentences about you, your family or your friends – when you use words in sentences about things people you know have done, the words are easier to remember

b funny sentences – a funny image can help the word stay in your memory

c sentences that explain the word – these make the meaning clear, like the examples in dictionaries

Here are some of my latest examples. Can you guess which types they are?

1 I prefer **plain** T-shirts to ones with writing or pictures on them.

2 Your skin gets **sweaty** when you're hot or exercise a lot.

3 My baby brother always wipes his nose on his **sleeve**.

4 The giraffe couldn't **do up** the zip on his jacket because it was too long!

5 A **checked** pattern is a pattern of squares of different colours.

6 I thought I saw a zebra – but it was a horse in a black and white **striped** T-shirt.

So … that's all from me today. Don't forget to share some example sentences of your own. You can post them below!

2 **Match Ela's examples 1–6 with types a–c.**

1 ______ 4 ______

2 ______ 5 ______

3 ______ 6 ______

OWN IT!

3 **Choose five words from the box and write an example sentence for each one. Use all of Ela's types a–c at least once.**

baggy	charge	fashion victim	flat	hang up	high-heeled	laces	not go with	spotted	updates

1 ______________________________

____

2 ______________________________

____

3 ______________________________

____

4 ______________________________

____

5 ______________________________

____

4 **Tell your partner your sentences from Exercise 3. Which types a–c are they? Which sentences are your favourites and why?**

2 CHANGES

LEARNING OUTCOMES

I can ...

- understand texts about international exchanges and a mystery object
- explain how to use something
- write an opinion essay
- understand how to use *used to* and *would* for past habits, the past simple, and the past perfect with *never, already, by (then), by the time*
- talk about changes and parts of objects
- practise learning new words by using them in different situations and identifying key words to understand audio texts
- make a history exhibition.

Start it!

1 Look at the photo. Do you know what this animal is, and how it changes?

2 Before you watch, how do you think cities change over time?

3 Which two events changed the city of Seoul? Watch and check.

4 How has your town or city changed?

Watch video 2.1

p25

Language in action 2.2

p27

Language in action 2.3

p28

Everyday English 2.4

VOCABULARY
Phrasal verbs: changes

1 **Which of the phrases a–l describes picture 1? Which phrase describes picture 2?**

a **settle down** in a new school
b **look forward to** the weekend
c **sign up** for French lessons
d **try out** a new restaurant
e **turn out** well
f **move out** of a house
g **move to** a new school
h **go back** to the beginning
i **end up** in the wrong place
j **go through** a hard time
k **do without** the Internet
l **turn down** an invitation

1

2

2.01 **2** **Match definitions 1–12 with the phrasal verbs a–l in Exercise 1. Listen, check and repeat.**

1 feel happy about something in the future b
2 not have something
3 finally be in a place/situation
4 experience
5 stop living in a particular place
6 try something new
7 start to feel happy in a new place/situation
8 return
9 join an organised activity
10 say no to something
11 have a particular result
12 change to

2.02 **3** **Listen to six conversations and complete the sentences using the phrases in Exercise 1.**

1 Mr Smith decides to ______________ for French classes.
2 Molly ______________ the baseball game. Ben ______________ to the game.
3 Tom is ______________ at the moment. He ______________ new school.
4 Jo asks Ed to ______________ the beginning.
5 The girls are going to ______________ restaurant.
6 In the end, Leila's party ______________ .

LEARN TO LEARN
Using words in different situations

Using new words in different situations helps you to remember them.

4 **Think of different situations for the phrasal verbs in Exercise 1.**

What can you look forward to?

A party ... the end of exams ...

Use it!

5 **Think of questions using the phrasal verbs in Exercise 1. Ask and answer.**

Have you tried out a new restaurant recently?

Yes. We went to a great Italian restaurant last week.

Explore it!

Guess the correct answer.

Where do most international students come from?

a USA b China c India

Find out a fact about students in your country. Write a question for your partner.

ACE EXCHANGES – DISCOVER A NEW WORLD AND A NEW YOU!

Student testimonials

LUCY

I love school here – it's so different to the USA. Students have almost no homework and very few exams. At my school, we don't even have school subjects. We study topics and do projects instead. It's a great way to learn.

This experience has really helped me to become more confident. I didn't use to be adventurous, but I've tried lots of new things since I arrived here eight months ago. For example, I went on a reindeer safari on my birthday, and I've been going ice-swimming every Saturday. Plus, I've made lots of friends. Finns are very cool people.

It hasn't all been easy. Winter is very hard because it's really dark – there are only three or four hours of light every day. The good thing is that you can see the beautiful Northern Lights.

If you get the opportunity to study abroad don't turn it down, especially not if you can come to Finland!

BEN

Last year I spent six wonderful months in Mexico. I used to dream about living in a different country, so when I discovered Ace Exchanges I signed up immediately. It was an absolutely incredible experience. I loved the mix of local, European and African cultures, and the people were really outgoing.

Of course, I went through some ups and downs at first, especially dealing with a different school system. For example, many Mexican schools have two timetables. Some students start school at 7.30 am and some – like me – start at 2 pm. We would finish at 8 pm! Also, I didn't speak much Spanish when I arrived, so it was quite difficult to follow lessons. But my classmates would always help me, and I improved a lot.

I felt a bit homesick from time to time, but now I feel like I have two homes. In fact, I've decided to go to university there. I'm really looking forward to going back.

READING

A brochure

1 **Look at the photos. Which show Finland? Which show Mexico? What do you think it is like to live there?**

2.03 **2** **Read the brochure. Write *L* (Lucy) or *B* (Ben).**

Which person …

1. has been abroad for more than half a year? ___
2. found the country's education system difficult? ___
3. has changed in a positive way? ___
4. found part of the year difficult because of the light? ___
5. likes the variety of cultures? ___
6. can do something better than they used to do? ___

3 **Find words in the brochure that mean:**

1. happy to try new things (Lucy) ________
2. from the nearby area (Ben) ________
3. friendly and sociable (Ben) ________
4. a mix of good and bad experiences (Ben) ________
5. missing your family (Ben) ________

4 **Read the sentences and write *T* (true), *F* (false) or *DS* (doesn't say).**

1. In Finland, students never do exams. F
2. Students have long breaks in Finland. ___
3. Lucy has been ice-swimming more than once. ___
4. Ben never wanted to leave the USA. ___
5. Mexican students don't all finish school at the same time. ___
6. Ben wants to go back home soon. ___

Voice it!

5 **Discuss the questions.**

1. Can you think of a country you would like to go on an exchange to?
2. Why would you like to visit that country?
3. What do you think would be difficult about living there?

Finished? p119 Ex 1

LANGUAGE IN ACTION
used to, *would* and past simple

Watch video 2.2
What did her grandmother use to write on?
What did she use to do outdoors?

used to / would	Past simple
I [1]________ **to** dream about living in a different country.	I **went** on a reindeer safari.
I **didn't** [2]________ **to** be adventurous.	I **didn't speak** much Spanish.
Did Lucy [3]________ **to** be adventurous?	**Did** Ben **learn** a lot of Spanish?
My classmates [4]________ always help me.	

Pronunciation p141

1 **Complete the examples in the table above with one word in each gap. Use the brochure on page 24 to help you.**

2 **Complete the rules with *used to/would* or the past simple.**

1 We use __________ to talk about situations that continued and actions that happened more than once in the past.
2 We use __________ to talk about things that happened only once.

3 **Complete the text with *used to* and the verbs in brackets.**

My grandfather's childhood was different to mine. When he was a boy, he never [1]used to have (have) many toys, but he [2]__________ (have) a lot of time. He [3]__________ (love) playing outside. Sometimes, his friends [4]__________ (play) outside all day – they [5]__________ (go) out early and then they [6]__________ (come) home late at night. I think it [7]__________ (be) safer for children then.

Get it right!

We don't use ***would*** with past situations, only repeated actions.

*We **used to** live in Murcia.*

NOT ~~*We would live in Murcia.*~~

*We **used to / would** play tennis at school.*

4 **Circle the correct words. Sometimes both are possible.**

1 More people *would / used to* live in the countryside than in cities. Now it's the opposite.
2 In the past, TV channels *would / used to* stop at night.
3 Some people *didn't use to / wouldn't* smile in photos because their teeth were bad.
4 Many people *would / used to* think that the Earth was flat.

5 **Complete the sentences with *used to*, *didn't use to* or the past simple and the verbs in brackets.**

1 For his birthday, Aidan got (get) a new bike. He loved it.
2 Ada __________ (like) apples much, but now she does.
3 I __________ (end up) in the wrong place yesterday because I didn't have a map.
4 When Bill was younger, he __________ (turn down) invitations all the time because he was so shy.

Use it!

6 **Write questions for a partner about their parents' lives with *used to* or the past simple.**

1 what toys / play with __________
2 study English / at school __________
3 how / meet __________

7 **Ask and answer the questions.**

What toys did your parents use to play with?

I think they used to play with wooden toys, and they would often play outside.

Finished? p119 Ex 2

VOCABULARY AND LISTENING

Parts of objects

1 Look at the photos. Which objects do you recognise?

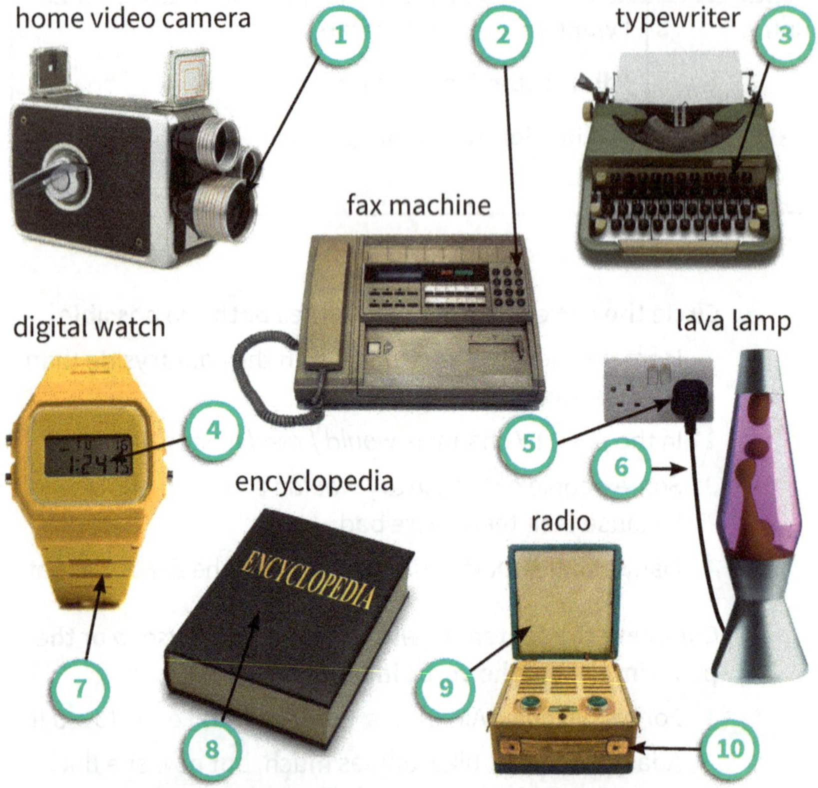

2.08 **2 Match the words in the box with parts of the objects 1–10. Listen, check and repeat.**

button ☐	cable ☐	cover ☐	display ☐	handle ☐
key ☐	lens 1	lid ☐	plug ☐	strap ☐

2.09 **3 Circle the correct words. Listen and check.**

1 When you carry a backpack, do you use one *strap / cable* or both? Why?
2 Do you always put the *handle / lid* back on the toothpaste after using it?
3 How often do you clean the *key / lens* of the camera on your phone?
4 Without looking, can you remember what is on the *cover / display* of this book?
5 Can you name six objects that have an on/off *plug / button*?
6 Do you take your phone charger *cable / display* with you when you go out?

Use it!

4 Ask and answer the questions in Exercise 3. Are your answers similar or different?

A quiz show

2.10 **5 Listen to a quiz show about retro objects. Which three objects in Exercise 1 are mentioned?**

LEARN TO LEARN

Identifying key words

Identifying key words before you listen can help you understand what you hear.

6 Read the questions and the options and underline the key words.

1 Joey pushes the buzzer too early because he …
   a can't wait to play.
   b doesn't understand the rules.
2 Nicola guesses the first object correctly because she …
   a has seen one before.
   b has heard of it before.
3 People had fax machines …
   a in their houses.
   b in their workplaces.
4 People used lava lamps …
   a instead of lightbulbs.
   b because they were attractive.

2.10 **7 Listen again and answer the questions in Exercise 6.**

Voice it!

8 Discuss the questions.

1 Do you know any retro objects that have come back into fashion?
2 What do you think of them?

LANGUAGE IN ACTION

Past perfect with *never, already, by (then), by the time*

Watch video 2.3
Where did she go last week?
When were 3-D printers first developed?

This was before anyone **had** [1] ________ **heard** of printers.
I'**d heard** of fax machines before, but I'**d** [2] ________ **seen** one.
They'**d** [3] ________ **gone** out of fashion **by the time** you were born.
I **hadn't started** yet.
Had you [4] ________ **seen** a digital watch before then?

1 **Complete the examples in the table above with *already*, *ever* or *never*.**

2 **Circle the correct words to complete the rules.**

1. ***Already***, ***never*** and ***ever*** come *before* / *after* the main verb.
2. ***By the time*** means *before* / *after* something happened.

3 **Answer the questions with the past perfect.**

1. How did you know what would happen in the film? (already / read / the book)
   Because I had already read the book.
2. Why did you get lost? (never / be / there before)
   ____
3. Did you get a ticket for the concert? No, (by the time / I went online / they / sell out)
   ____
4. How was the party? (already / finish / when we got there)
   ____

2.11 **4** **Complete the text with the past simple or the past perfect. Listen and check.**

> Last year I [1] went (go) on an exchange to Moscow. I [2] ________ (never / travel) alone before, so I [3] ________ (feel) nervous at first. Before I [4] ________ (go), I [5] ________ (already / learn) to read the Russian alphabet, although I [6] ________ (not practise) speaking Russian. By the time I [7] ________ (leave), I [8] ________ (improve) a lot. Everybody in Moscow [9] ________ (be) really kind and friendly, but it [10] ________ (not be) easy to deal with the cold weather. I [11] ________ (not pack) enough warm clothes, so I had to buy some after I [12] ________ (arrive). Anyway, I can't wait to go back. I [13] ________ (not expect) to enjoy it much before I actually [14] ________ (get) there, but in the end I really [15] ________ (do)!

Use it!

5 **Ask and answer the questions about the topics below. Use the past perfect.**

1. hear of / connected clothing?
2. see / a picture of 3-D printed clothes?
3. hear of / ice-swimming?
4. see / a picture of the Northern Lights?

Before you started using this book, had you ever heard of connected clothing?

No, I'd never heard of it, but now I want to know more! / Yes, I had. I'd already read about it online.

Finished? p119 Ex 3

SPEAKING

Explaining how to use something

2.12 **1 Listen to the conversation. Which of the things in the box does the typewriter have?**

cable	display	ink	keys	plug	speaker

YUSUF What's that? [1] Is it some kind of computer?
MERI No, it's my grandad's old typewriter.
YUSUF Where's the display?
MERI There isn't one, and there's no plug or cable.
YUSUF That's so old-school! How did it work?
MERI The paper would move as you typed. [2] ______________ press the keys hard, but not too fast or they get stuck. Try it out!
YUSUF [3] ______________
MERI That's it. Just imagine – people used to type books on these things!
YUSUF No way! I can't even find the letters I want.
MERI You need to sign up for typing classes! They're in the same place as an ordinary keyboard.
YUSUF Oh no! [4] ______________ How do I go back? There's no 'delete' key.
MERI [5] ______________ start all over again.
YUSUF No, thanks! Anyway, how come your grandad had this?
MERI He used to need it for work, but after a while he ended up buying a computer.
YUSUF I'm not surprised! I'm glad they'd invented computers by the time I started school! I'd hate to do my homework on this!

2.12 **2 Complete the conversation with the phrases from the *Useful language* box. Listen and check.**

Useful language

Is it some kind of ...? I've messed it up.
Like this, you mean? What you do is, you ...
You'll have to ...

Watch video 2.4
Everyday English

all over again
I'm not surprised.
old-school That's it.

3 Complete the sentences with the phrases in the *Everyday English* box.

1 Barry's not here yet. ______________ – he's always late.
2 A Do I press this button here?
B ______________
3 Your new jacket's so ______________. My dad used to have one like that.
4 Oh no! I've lost my homework! I'll have to do it ______________.

PLAN

4 Choose one of the objects on page 26. Make notes on how to use it.

SPEAK

5 Practise the explanation with your partner. Remember to use past tenses, vocabulary from this unit and phrases from the *Useful language* and *Everyday English* boxes.

CHECK

6 Work with another pair. Listen to their explanation and complete the notes.

How does the object work? ______________
____
Do you understand how to use it? ______________
____

WRITING
An opinion essay

1 In what ways has life changed for teenagers in the last 30 years?

2 Read the essay. Does it mention any of your ideas in Exercise 1?

Are teenagers today more or less stressed than previous generations?

The world has changed a great deal in the last few decades, especially for teenagers, and not always in a positive way. In particular, people of my generation are a lot more stressed than teenagers in the past.

Firstly, we are under enormous pressure to do well in exams. This means that we spend a lot of time studying. Young people didn't use to study as much because it wasn't always necessary to go to university. Therefore, they had more time to relax and hang out with friends.

Secondly, previous generations didn't have online profiles to worry about. In fact, young people 20 or 30 years ago hadn't even heard of 'followers' and 'likes' because social media hadn't been invented yet. For people of my age, it is almost impossible to do without social media. In addition, it can become extremely addictive.

In conclusion, I would say that teenagers today have more stressful lives than our parents did.

3 Complete the table with the linkers from the *Useful language* box. Look at the linkers in the essay to help you.

Order of ideas	Connection between ideas
firstly	

Useful language

firstly in addition in conclusion secondly therefore this means that

4 Complete the essay with the linkers from the *Useful language* box. Do you agree with the writer? Sometimes there is more than one possible answer.

Some people think that online games are worse for you than traditional games, because they are addictive and don't involve physical exercise, but is this always true?

In my opinion, online games have many good points. [1]Firstly, they improve your memory and your problem-solving skills.

[2]________, you can make friends. [3]________, you play with people from around the world.
[4]________ you often have to communicate in English and [5]________ your English improves.
However, it's important to spend time with your friends offline.

[6]________, online games can be unhealthy, but only if you spend all your time playing them.

Write an opinion essay.

PLAN

5 Look at the statement and make notes.

> Teenagers today have more freedom than in the past.

Do you agree or disagree with the statement?

Write two reasons for your opinion.

Give a summary of your opinion.

WRITE

6 Write your opinion essay. Remember to include, *used to*, the past simple and past perfect and phrases from the *Useful language* box.

CHECK

7 Do you …
- give your opinion?
- give reasons for your opinion?
- summarise your opinion?

Finished? p119 Ex 4

THE HISTORY PROJECT

1 FASHION

Fashion is always changing, and old styles often come back into fashion, although few people look forward to seeing 1970s fashion again. If you watch TV shows from that decade, you will see that people used to wear trousers that were tight at the top and wide at the bottom, flowery dresses, a lot of tight cotton T-shirts or shirts with big collars, and plenty of big round glasses. During the early 1970s, bright colours were extremely trendy, but by the end of the decade they had almost completely disappeared. Black, white, grey and brown had replaced them, although people still wore enormous glasses.

2 TECHNOLOGY

It is hard to imagine dealing with the ups and downs of modern life without computers and smartphones. However, in the 70s there were very few computers, and the ones that existed were a lot bigger than those we have today. They were far slower, with simple displays and enormous buttons. Compared to the devices we use today, they also had very little memory. In fact, the computers on the Apollo spaceships that took men to the moon had less memory than some modern toasters. By the beginning of the 1970s, some companies had started to use computers in their offices, but it was extremely rare to see a computer in a house. In fact, most people had never used one, and some people had never seen one.

A retro museum exhibition

1 Look at the photos. What period in history do you think they are from?

2 (2.13) Read the exhibit labels. Which one do you find most interesting? Why?

3 Complete the table about exhibits 2 and 3.

	1	2	3
Area	fashion	technology	music
Period	1970s		
Examples	trousers (tight at top, baggy at bottom), flowery dresses, big glasses, bright colours		
Changes over time	black, white, grey, brown became more popular		

3 MUSIC

Music has always been an important part of teenage identity, but in an age of streaming and downloading it's easy to forget that it hasn't always been as available as it is today. In the 1970s young music fans would spend hours in record shops looking for new music to buy. It wasn't only the music that was popular. The record covers were also important, and many of them became famous for their artwork. By the middle of the 1990s, CDs had become more popular than records. Nevertheless, people continued to collect records and DJs still used to play them at discos. Recently, they have come back into fashion, as many people prefer the sound of a record to the sound of a digital file.

How to schedule

4 **Ask your teacher how long you have to complete the project. Then decide together how long to spend on each of these stages:**

1. looking for information and photos
2. writing draft texts for the labels
3. checking and correcting the drafts
4. writing the final labels and putting them on a poster with the photos.

PLAN

5 **Work in groups. Complete the steps below.**

- Decide which period in history you want to concentrate on (for example, the 19th century, the 1980s).
- Choose three areas you want to focus on.

entertainment fashion food and drink
house and home school life
technology/communication toys and games

- Decide who is going to research and write about which exhibit.

PRESENT

6 **Present your history exhibition on the wall of your classroom. Remember to include a title for each label, vocabulary from this unit, *used to*, the past simple and past perfect and the tips in *How to* schedule.**

CHECK

7 **Read the other groups' history exhibitions. What areas are they focusing on? Which group's exhibition is most interesting?**

2 REVIEW

VOCABULARY

1 Complete the conversation with the correct form of a phrasal verb.

A How was your bike trip? Where did you go?

B Well, we wanted to [1]________ a new route. We were planning to cycle to this old village near the sea, but we got lost and [2]________ on a farm!

A Didn't you have a map with you?

B No, but the farmer helped us, so it [3]________ OK in the end. We found the village!

A Was it nice there?

B Beautiful. I'd love to [4]________ one day. How was your weekend?

A Not great. I was sick. My friends wanted me to go a concert. I'd said yes, and I [5]________ to it, but in the end I had to [6]________ them ________.

2 Circle the correct words.

Did you know ... ?

- The [1]*lids / covers* of plastic water bottles are made from a different plastic to the bottle.
- If you change the [2]*lens / display* on your phone to black and white, it can become less addictive.
- On old trains, you couldn't open the doors with a [3]*button / plug*. You had to use a [4]*strap / handle*, like a normal door.
- Every second, 600,000 people around the world press the space [5]*cable / key* when they're on a computer.

LANGUAGE IN ACTION

3 Complete the text with *used to*, *would* or the past simple and the verb in brackets. Sometimes there is more than one possible answer.

My dad's a writer now, although he [1]____________ (not be). He [2]____________ (be) a diplomat, so when I was small, my family [3]____________ (move) countries all the time. Once, we [4]____________ (live) in three different countries in two years! I remember when I [5]____________ (move) to the school where I am now, in Rio de Janeiro. I [6]____________ (not know) any Portuguese at first, so the first week [7]____________ (be) difficult. I used to take my lunch to the playground and then I [8]____________ (eat) it alone. However, Brazilian people are really friendly, so after a few days my classmates [9]____________ (start) to invite me to eat with them and I quickly [10]____________ (make) lots of friends. We've been living here for many years now, and I'm really happy.

4 Complete Ben's message to Tom with the past perfect.

Tom, I'm so sorry I missed the wedding! I decided to take the car to the airport, but because I [1]__________ (never / drive) there before, I got lost. Just the night before, I [2]__________ (think), 'I must fix the GPS!', but then I completely forgot! Anyway, I got to the airport around two o'clock. The plane [3]__________ (not taken off), but by the time I finished checking in, the gate [4]__________ (close). I tried to buy a ticket for the next flight, but they [5]__________ (already / sell out)!

Self-assessment

I can use phrasal verbs to talk about changes.

I can use words to talk about parts of objects.

I can use *used to*, *would* and the past simple.

I can use the past perfect with *never*, *already*, *by (then)*, *by the time*.

LEARN TO LEARN

LEARN TO ... HELP YOUR PARTNER IMPROVE THEIR WRITING

When you write something, ask your partner to check it. You can improve your writing this way.

1 **Read the instructions for the writing task. Correct Edison's mistakes to help him improve.**

WRITING TASK

Write about a favourite toy or game from your childhood.

- Write between 100 and 130 words.
- Use language from this unit.

Don't forget to use punctuation and check your spelling!

When I was little, I [1]~~use~~ used to play with Lego® bricks all the time. I would [2]building ________ all kinds of things – cars, [3]airplaynes ________, houses. I even built a computer with keys and a display. After I finished one thing, I would keep it and then try out something else, but I once [4]used to build ________ a ship that I kept for weeks. [5]I've ________ never built anything like it before. However, I remember my mum [6]would be ________ really angry with me one day because I played with it in the bathroom and ended up damaging the sides of the bath. I've still got a photo of it somewhere [7]‸ ________

Number of words: 107

2 **Answer the questions in the checklist. Has Edison completed the task in Exercise 1?**

Checklist		
	Edison's writing	**w**
Has he/she ...		
1 written about the topic?	Yes / No	Yes / No
2 written between 100 and 130 words?	Yes / No	Yes / No
3 used phrasal verbs for changes and words for parts of objects?	Yes / No	Yes / No
4 added details to make it interesting?	Yes / No	Yes / No
How well has he/she used ...		
5 the past simple?	☹ 😐 ☺	☹ 😐 ☺
6 *used to* and *would*?	☹ 😐 ☺	☹ 😐 ☺
7 the past perfect?	☹ 😐 ☺	☹ 😐 ☺
8 punctuation?	☹ 😐 ☺	☹ 😐 ☺
9 correct spelling?	☹ 😐 ☺	☹ 😐 ☺
Other comments?	*I enjoyed the part about your mum being angry!*	

OWN IT!

3 **Do the writing task in Exercise 1.**

4 **Answer the questions in the checklist for your partner's writing.**

5 **Tell your partner what you like and what they can improve.**

3 FOOD FOR THOUGHT

LEARNING OUTCOMES

I can ...

- understand texts from an online forum and a cooking show
- give cooking instructions
- write a listicle
- understand how to use different future forms
- talk about cooking and quantities
- make adjectives from verbs, use diagrams, and understand words from context by using the rest of the text.

Start it!

1. Look at the photo. Would you like to eat this food? Why? / Why not?
2. Before you watch, how do you think food has changed in the last 100 years?
3. What two foods will we eat more of in the future? Watch and check.
4. Are there other ways that our eating habits may change in the future?

Watch video 3.1

p37

Language in action 3.2

p39

Language in action 3.3

p40

Everyday English 3.4

p42

Globetrotters 3.5

VOCABULARY
Cooking verbs

3.01 **1 Match the verbs in the box with photos 1–12. Listen, check and repeat.**

bake	1	chop		fry	
grate		grill		heat	
overcook		peel		roast	
season		slice		spread	

3.02 **2 Circle the correct verbs to complete the instructions to make a homemade pizza. Listen and check.**

[1]*Spread* / *Peel* the tomatoes and [2]*chop* / *overcook* them. Then [3]*bake* / *heat* them in a pan and [4]*slice* / *season* with salt and pepper. [5]*Grill* / *Roast* some bread. Then [6]*fry* / *spread* the tomatoes on the bread and [7]*grate* / *season* some cheese on top. [8]*Fry* / *Bake* in the oven, but only for a few minutes – you don't want to [9]*overcook* / *slice* it!

3 Circle the verb which does not go with each food.

1 pepper: chop fry spread
2 bread: bake roast slice
3 chicken: heat overcook grate
4 fish: peel grill season

LEARN TO LEARN
Wordbuilding: adjectives from verbs

Learn the adjective form of new verbs. Sometimes the form is similar, for example *bake* (v) *baked* (adj).

4 Write the adjective form of the verbs in Exercise 1.

bake *baked*	overcook ______
chop ______	peel ______
fry ______	roast ______
grate ______	season ______
grill ______	slice ______
heat ______	spread ______

5 Which verbs in Exercise 1 usually go with the foods in the box?

apple bread cheese chicken chocolate egg jam meat tomato pepper

Grate … You can have grated apple, cheese, chocolate, egg, tomato and pepper.

Use it!

6 Discuss the questions.

1 Do you usually eat grilled, fried, baked or roast foods? Which are your favourites?
2 What can you cook?
3 Is it important to know how to cook? Why?

Explore it!

Guess the correct answer.

During the Chinese mid-autumn festival, people traditionally bake mooncakes. Which ingredient is baked inside them to symbolise the moon?

a chicken egg b ostrich egg c duck egg

Find another fact about a traditional food. Write a question for your partner.

Pronunciation p141

READING

An online forum

1 What types of food can you see in the photos? Which ones would you eat?

2 Read the forum and match comments 1–5 with photos A–E. 3.05

1 ______ 3 ______ 5 ______
2 ______ 4 ______

3 Read the forum again and match the future food solutions 1–5 with the reasons a–e.

Future food solution	Why it solves the problem
1 Jellyfish	a cheap and already eaten in many parts of the world
2 Lab food	b can make new food from old
3 Smart fridges	c better for the environment
4 3-D printers	d help us use the food we already have so we don't buy food we don't need
5 Insects	e a new food and we need to find more of these

4 Match the words in **bold** in the forum with the meanings.

1 another possibility ______
2 the taste of something ______
3 not real ______
4 something special and good to eat ______
5 cooking instructions ______

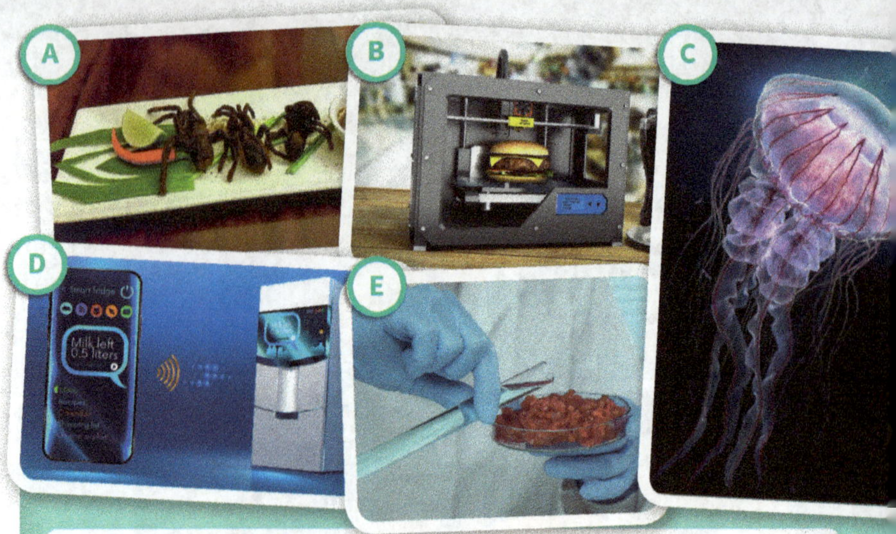

CLASS 4C STUDY ROOM

Read the article about future food and add your comments. Professor Jones is coming to Friday's class and we're going to discuss your ideas.

1 There isn't going to be enough food for everyone in the future because the population is growing, so we're going to need to be more adventurous and find new foods. I read that we could actually eat jellyfish, although many people won't like the idea. Jellyfish probably doesn't have much **flavour**, but if you season it and roast it, it might be quite tasty! ***Abi***

2 We may eat **artificial** fish or meat grown in a laboratory in the future. I think the idea sounds disgusting, but scientists say it will be better for the planet. I'm definitely not going to eat lab burgers! ***Ben***

3 We throw away far too much food, often because we buy more than we need. I read about these cool apps that will tell us what's in the fridge and suggest **recipes** with the food we already have so we don't waste so much. I think they'll be really popular. ***Dana***

4 One thing I'm not sure about is 3-D printed food. The idea that a printer will produce our food is a bit strange. But people say we'll be able to print snacks from food we're going to throw away, so 3-D printers might help reduce food waste. ***Marco***

5 Experts say that meat will be far more expensive in the future, so we're going to have to eat **alternative** types of food. Insects are cheaper than farm animals, so they may be a solution. Grilled grasshoppers are a popular snack in Mexico and fried tarantulas are a **delicacy** in Cambodia. In fact, lots of cultures eat bugs, so why can't we? ***Emma***

Voice it!

5 Discuss the questions.

1 Which of the ideas in Exercise 3 are your most and least favourite. Why?
2 What other future food solutions can you think of?

Finished? p120 Ex 1

LANGUAGE IN ACTION

Future tenses

Watch video 3.2
What's happening this Saturday?
Which workshop might he go to?

Present tenses and *be going to* for future plans and intentions
Friday's class **starts** at nine o'clock.
Professor Jones [1] ______ **coming** to Friday's class.
We**'re** [2] ______ discuss your ideas on Friday.

1 **Complete the examples in the table above. Use the online forum on page 36 to help you.**

2 **Circle the correct words to complete the conversation.**

A [1]*Do you / Are you going to* watch the final tonight?
B Yeah. Kate [2]*comes / is coming* to my house to watch it.
A What time [3]*does it start / is it starting*?
B 8 pm, but she [4]*comes / is going to come* at 7 pm.

Get it right!

We often use the present continuous or *be going to* to talk about the future.

*John's **cooking** later.* **OR** *John's **going to cook** later.*

Predictions with *be going to, will* and *may/might*
The population is growing, so we [1] ______ need to find new foods. (a future prediction based on evidence)
We [2] ______ eat artificial fish or meat. (a future prediction we are not sure about)
Experts say that meat [3] ______ be far more expensive. (a prediction we are sure about)

3 **Complete the examples in the table above. Use the online forum on page 36 to help you.**

4 **Read the leaflet. Complete the dialogue with the present simple, present continuous, *be going to*, *will* or *may/might* form of the verbs in brackets.**

LUCAS Hey Milena, [1] are you coming (come) to Abi's birthday tomorrow?
MILENA Where [2] ______ you ______ (go)?
LUCAS To 'Dining in the Dark'. We [3] ______ (have) dinner in darkness!
MILENA That's strange. Abi [4] ______ (not like) it!
LUCAS I'm sure she [5] ______ (love) it! It [6] ______ (be) different to anything she's done before.
MILENA But you [7] ______ (not be able to) see the food. You [8] ______ (eat) something you don't like.
LUCAS I know! We [9] ______ (have to) guess what we're eating!
MILENA What time [10] ______ it ______ (start)?
LUCAS At eight o'clock.
MILENA I'm not sure. I [11] ______ (come). I [12] ______ (tell) you later.

Use it!

5 **Write the questions. Use future tenses. Ask and answer.**

1 What / you / do / tomorrow?
______
2 How old / you / be / in 2050?
______
3 What foods / we / eat / in the future?
______
4 When / your next class / start?
______

What are you going to do tomorrow?

I'm not sure. I might go to the beach.

Finished? p120 Ex 2

LISTENING AND VOCABULARY

Quantities

3.06 **1** **Read the recipe and choose the correct photo 1–3. Listen and repeat.**

1 

2 

3 

How to make your own fruity cereal

Mix the following ingredients in a bowl:

- a cup of cereal, like oats
- some pieces of strawberry
- some slices of banana
- some chunks of pineapple
- a handful of blueberries
- a packet of nuts
- a pinch of cinnamon
- a sprinkle of brown sugar

Serve with a spoonful of yoghurt or a splash of milk.

Nutritious and delicious!

2 **Complete the sentences with quantities in Exercise 1 in the singular or plural form.**

1 I have two *slices* toast for breakfast and ______ coffee with ______ milk.
2 If your throat hurts, have ______ honey.
3 Season the pasta sauce with ______ salt and pepper.
4 I'm going to have a ______ crisps for lunch.
5 I love cookies with big ______ chocolate!
6 I make the best Greek salad. I put in ______ olives, some ______ feta cheese and ______ oregano on top.

LEARN TO LEARN

Using diagrams

Use diagrams to help remember new phrases.

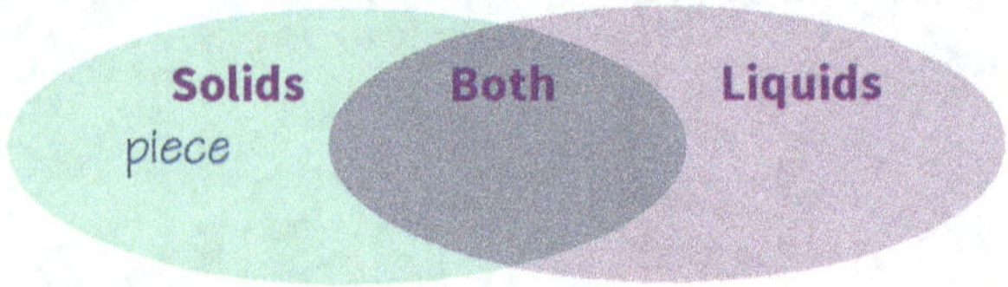

3 **Add quantities in Exercise 1 to the diagram.**

Use it!

4 **Think of a food you like and tell your partner the ingredients.**

A pancake … You need two cups of flour …

A recipe

3.07 **5** **Listen to the cooking show and write the quantities.**

Pear smoothie	Ant tacos
1 ______ orange juice	6 ______ ant larvae
2 ______ chopped pear	7 ______ chopped tomatoes
3 ______ cricket flour	8 ______ chopped chillies
4 ______ mango and pineapple	9 ______ salt and pepper
5 ______ lime juice	10 ______ chopped coriander

3.07 **6** **Listen again and circle the correct answers.**

1 Both of Anton's dishes … .
   a contain insects b are spicy c are Mexican
2 By 2030 there will be … billion people in the world.
   a 5.5 b 6.5 c 8.5
3 Cricket flour will add … to the smoothie.
   a fruit flavour b vitamins c protein
4 Anton is going to … the ant larvae.
   a fry b heat c roast

LANGUAGE IN ACTION

Future continuous and future perfect

Watch video 3.3
Who will be making our food in the future?
What food was invented by accident?

Future continuous	Future perfect
I [1] ________ **making** a pear smoothie.	We [2] ________ **seen** and **tasted** some very unusual dishes
We [3] ________ **eating** a lot of meat in the future.	He [4] ________ **finished** by the end of the programme.
What [5] ________ you ________ **making**?	[6] ________ you ________ **finished** by the end of the programme?

Future continuous

1 **Complete the examples in the table above with *will/won't be* or *will/won't have*.**

2 **Complete the sentences with the future continuous form.**

eat   not see   stay   ~~sleep~~

1. Don't ring me at 8.30. I'll be sleeping.
2. Where ________ they ________ while they're on holiday?
3. I've got exams next week. I ________ my friends.
4. ________ we ________ insects in 30 years' time?

Future perfect

3 **Complete the sentences with the future perfect form.**

1. I think scientists will have found (find) life on other planets by 2060.
2. I ________ (not finish) my exams by the end of May.
3. They ________ (not start) yet. It's only 7.30.

3.08 **4** **Complete the conversation with the future continuous or perfect form of the verbs. Listen and check.**

ZOE How [1] will restaurants have changed (change) by 2030?
SAM I think they [2] ________ (become) more automatic. Instead of human chefs, machines [3] ________ (cook) your food and human waiters [4] ________ (not serve) the tables, robots will.
ZOE So humans [5] ________ (not work) in restaurants?
SAM That's right, but I think we [6] ________ (design) robots that look like humans by then.

Use it!

5 **Write sentences about your future. Use the future continuous or perfect.**

In one years' time …
In 2050 …
On my 21st birthday …
By the end of this year …
By 2030 …
By the time I'm 25 …

In 2050 I'll be living in my own house.
By the time I'm 25 I'll have learned how to drive.

6 **Tell your partner your sentences about the future, but change some so that they are false. Can they guess which sentences are true and which are false?**

In 2050 I won't be living in my own house.

False?

Yes, it's false.

Finished? p120 Ex 3

SPEAKING

Giving instructions

3.09 **1 What can you see in the photo? What ingredients do you need to make it? Listen and check your answers.**

3.09 **2 Complete the conversation with the phrases from the *Useful language* box. Listen and check.**

ROB Can you give me the recipe for your yummy Spanish omelette? I'm going to make it for the picnic tomorrow. It won't take ages, will it?
EVA No, it's a piece of cake! [1] *You'll need* half a kilogramme of potatoes, five eggs, salt, oil and an onion.
ROB OK. Is that it?
EVA Yep, so [2] ________ peeling and slicing the potatoes. [3] ________, chop the onion.
ROB OK. Then what?
EVA Heat a cup of oil in a pan and fry the potatoes and onions.
ROB That's a fair amount of oil!
EVA Yeah, I know! [4] ________ frying, mix the eggs in a bowl. Then put everything together and add a pinch of salt. Heat a spoonful of oil in a smaller pan and pour in the mixture. Once the bottom part has cooked, [5] ________ flip the omelette with a plate and cook the other side.
ROB OK, I'll try.
EVA It's delicious! Your friends will all be asking for the recipe! Will you still be there at four?
ROB Yeah, but we'll have finished the omelette by then!

Useful language

Don't forget to … (+ verb)	While that's … (+ *-ing*)
Once that's done, …	You'll need …
Start by … (+ *-ing*)	

3 Match the phrases in the conversation with the meanings. How do you say these phrases in your language?

1 something that's easy ________
2 delicious ________
3 Is that everything? ________
4 quite a lot ________
5 a long time ________

Watch video 3.4
Everyday English

a fair amount   ages   a piece of cake
Is that it?   yummy

PLAN

4 Write about a recipe and the ingredients you need.

____
____
____

SPEAK

5 Practise explaining the recipe to your partner. Remember to use future tenses, vocabulary from this unit and phrases from the *Useful language* and *Everyday English* boxes.

CHECK

6 Work with another pair. Listen to their conversation and complete the notes.

What was the recipe for? ________
____
What ingredients do you need?
____
____
Would you like to eat this food?
____

WRITING
A listicle

1 What food can you see in the photos? Read Megan's listicle. Which of her predictions do you agree with?

2 The following are features of a good listicle. Which ones are in Megan's listicle?

1 an interesting title
2 a number in the title
3 short texts about the title, one for each number
4 some interesting predictions
5 photos

FIVE FOODS WE'LL ALL BE EATING IN 2070!

1 If there's one thing we'll still be eating in 50 years' time, it's pizza!
We've been eating pizza since the 19th century, so we're not going to stop now! In the future toppings will change for sure, but pizza isn't going anywhere!

2 Tasty meat alternatives
With more humans on the planet, we'll need alternative sources of protein such as insects. What could be tastier than a sprinkle of roast ants on your salad?

3 Classics that will never die out!
Some classic British dishes, like fish and chips, will be around forever, although the fish will probably come from fish farms instead of the sea.

4 Printed snacks
By 2070 we'll be printing most of our snacks with a 3-D printer. Impossible? Watch this space ...

5 Veggies and vegans
Vegetarian food is here to stay! In 2070 being veggie or vegan, and avoiding eggs, milk and cheese, will be the norm!

3 Read Megan's listicle again and make two lists.

Food that will be the same	Food that will be new
pizza	

4 Complete the *Useful language* phrases with the words in the box. Check in Megan's listicle.

anywhere forever norm space stay

Useful language

is here to [1] ______
isn't going [2] ______
Watch this [3] ______
will be around [4] ______
will be the [5] ______

Write your own listicle.

PLAN

5 Look at the questions and make notes.

1 What will people still be eating in 50 years' time?
2 What might we start eating in the future?
3 Which dishes will be around forever?
4 What food is unusual now but will be normal in the future?

WRITE

6 Write a listicle about your future food predictions. Remember to include future tenses, vocabulary from this unit and phrases from the *Useful language* box.

CHECK

7 Do you ...

- explain what we will or might be eating in the future?
- explain what will be normal in the future?
- make any other predictions?

Finished? p120 Ex 4

AROUND THE WORLD

READING
An article

Globetrotters

Watch video 3.5
Food in Japan

- What food is usually associated with your country or culture?
- Can you explain what *kaiseki* and *wagashi* are?
- How is Western food influencing Japanese food traditions?

3.10 **1 Look at the photos. What can you see? What do they tell you about food in Australia? Read the article and check your ideas.**

A TASTE OF Australia

A country's food is influenced by its inhabitants, geography, climate and wildlife, and Australia is no exception.

Traditional Australia

For thousands of years, the indigenous people of Australia have eaten plants and animals from the land or sea. Traditional Aboriginal food, or 'bush tucker', includes crocodile, emu and snake. Examples that are still eaten today include kangaroo, macadamia nuts and witchetty grubs. These tasty insect larvae are roasted on the fire or grilled on the barbecue!

Multicultural Australia

Since the first Europeans arrived in Australia over 200 years ago, people have been moving to the country from all over the world. As a result, Australian cuisine is multicultural and includes British, Italian, Greek and Asian food. Popular dishes are fish and chips, roast lamb and dim sum as well as traditional favourites such as kangaroo, seafood pizza and fried shark. The warm, sunny climate means plenty of fresh fruit and vegetables, and barbecues to grill meat or fish outside.

Tomorrow's Australia

Desert food

Australia has built the first farm in the world that can grow fruit and veg in a desert. The enormous solar-powered greenhouse only needs sunshine and seawater to work and Australia has plenty of both. The solar panels create enough energy to transform the salt water into fresh water which is used to water the tomato plants. It's strange to think that in the future we might be eating food which is grown in the desert.

Ugly food

Around a quarter of fruit and vegetables around the world is thrown away before it gets to the supermarkets because people believe it's too 'ugly' to sell. However, some Australian supermarkets are trying to sell this food. They tell their customers that even though the food looks odd, it tastes exactly the same as perfectly formed fruit and veg. There are lots of advantages to eating this ugly food. It's cheaper for customers, farmers sell more of their produce and we reduce food waste.

LEARN TO LEARN

Understanding words from context

When you see new words, use the rest of the sentence to help you understand them. Guess what the new word means and then check it in a dictionary.

2 **Find the words in the article and guess the meaning. Check in a dictionary or with your teacher.**

New word	What the other words tell me	What I think it means
1 indigenous	It's an adjective that describes people who have lived in Australia for a long time.	original, first
2 witchetty grubs		
3 multicultural		
4 shark		
5 solar-powered		
6 greenhouse		

3 **Read the article again and find examples of how these things influence Australia's food.**

Indigenous people

They have always eaten food from the land and sea and some is still eaten today, e.g. macadamia nuts and witchetty grubs.

Wildlife

______

______

People from other cultures

______

______

Climate

______

______

Food waste

______

______

4 **Find words in the article that mean:**

1 something not included in a group (introduction) ______
2 delicious (traditional Australia) ______
3 cooking (multicultural Australia) ______
4 a short word for vegetable (desert food) ______
5 strange (ugly food) ______

Voice it!

5 **Discuss the questions.**

1 Which foods from other cultures have become popular in your country?
2 Australia is adapting to changes by eating 'ugly' food. How else can we adapt what we eat or drink?

Explore it!

Guess the correct answer.

What will you not find on a pizza in Australia?

a emu b kangaroo c koala d crocodile

Find a fact about Australian food. Write a question for your partner to answer.

OWN IT! The Culture Project Teacher's Resource Bank

3 REVIEW

VOCABULARY

1 Circle the correct verbs.

1. *Season* / *Peel* the orange before you eat it.
2. Is there any butter to *spread* / *grate* on my toast?
3. Let's *roast* / *fry* a chicken in the oven.
4. Can I borrow a knife to *grill* / *slice* the tomato?
5. Sam *bakes* / *chops* his own bread. It's great!

2 Match the quantities with the photos. Then think of another example for each quantity.

chunk	☐	________	cup	☐	________
handful	☐	________	packet	☐	________
piece	☐	________	pinch	☐	________
slice	☐	________	splash	☐	________
spoonful	☐	________	sprinkle	☐	________

1

2

3

4

5

6

7

8

9

10

LANGUAGE IN ACTION

3 Circle the correct words to complete the conversation.

IVAN What [1]*do you* / *are you going* to do this afternoon?

ANDREA We [2]*'re going* / *will go* to the cinema. Juan and Ali [3]*come* / *are coming* too.

IVAN What film [4]*are you going to* / *will you* see?

ANDREA *The Scream Factor.*

IVAN But you hate horror films!

ANDREA I know! [5]*I'm not enjoying* / *I'm not going to enjoy* the film, but Ali wants to see it.

IVAN It [6]*might be* / *is* OK. Who knows, you [7]*won't* / *may* enjoy it.

ANDREA We'll see. Anyway, I have to go. It [8]*will start* / *starts* in 45 minutes.

4 Complete the predictions with the future continuous or perfect of the verbs in brackets. Which predictions do you agree / disagree with?

In 10 years' time …

1. African cuisine ________ (become) extremely popular.
2. most people ________ (stop) eating meat.
3. we ________ (not buy) 'ugly' fruit and veg.
4. we ________ (not go out) to restaurants. We ________ (order) food online to eat at home.

Self-assessment

I can use verbs to talk about food.

I can use words to talk about quantities.

I can use future tenses and *may/might*.

I can use the future continous and future perfect.

LEARN TO ... SET AND ACHIEVE LEARNING GOALS

When you know what your English learning goals are, you can take steps to achieve them.

1 **Read what Ada says about her learning goal. What is it? Has she achieved it yet?**

In three weeks' time I'm going to New Zealand with my brother. He doesn't speak English so I'll need to book the hotels, order food and ask directions. My goal is to learn enough travel English to do this. I've bought a book with useful phrases for tourists, and I've downloaded episodes of a podcast about New Zealand. I'm going to listen to one episode every week. I'm also going to learn one useful phrase from the book every day. Piece of cake!

2 **Write Ada's answers to questions 2–4.**

Action plan		NAME: Ada
1	What do I want to do?	learn enough travel English to book hotels, order food and ask directions
2	How much time do I have?	
3	How am I going to do it?	a ______ b ______
4	How often am I going to do the things in 3?	a ______ b ______
5	What's my goal in one sentence?	By the time we go to New Zealand, I'll have learned enough travel English.

3 **Read what Enzo says about his learning goal. Write his answers to questions 1 and 2.**

One month from now we've got a speaking exam. I want to get a good grade, but I'm not great at speaking – not like my sister. She speaks English really well!

NAME: Enzo	
1	
2	
3	a ______ b ______
4	a ______ b ______
5	

4 **Whose advice should Enzo take?**

Why don't you practise with your sister? Ten minutes a day would help. – **Ela**

I'd study lots of vocabulary the night before. And don't sleep! – **Hamid**

Look at the Everyday English phrases in our book. Use three of them every day. – **Olga**

5 **Use your answers in Exercise 4 to complete questions 3 and 4 of Enzo's action plan. Write one sentence about his goal for question 5.**

OWN IT!

6 **Think of an English learning goal. What are your answers to questions 1 to 5?**

7 **Tell your partner about your learning goal. Use the action plan to help you.**

4 SENSE AND SENSITIVITY

LEARNING OUTCOMES

I can ...

- understand texts about people who don't feel pain or fear and artists who make sound effects
- make guesses and give clues about unfamiliar objects
- write an encyclopaedia entry
- make deductions and express obligation, prohibition, necessity and advice
- talk about senses and describe how things look, sound and feel, etc.
- brainstorm and use visual clues when listening
- create an infographic.

Start it!

1 Look at the photo. What different senses do you use when you enjoy an ice cream?
2 Before you watch, what do you think bats, dolphins and submarines have in common?
3 Which animal has the best hearing and how does that help them? Watch and check.
4 Can you think of any other animals which have special senses?

Watch video 4.1

p49

Language in action 4.2

p51

Language in action 4.3

p52

Everyday English 4.4

VOCABULARY
The five senses

1 **Match the words in bold with photos A–E. Answer the questions.**

Have you ever:

1. seen a **durian**? ☐
2. touched a **snake**? ☐
3. played football on **artificial grass**? ☐
4. heard a **koala**? ☐
5. eaten a **knickerbocker glory**? ☐

2 **Match the questions in Exercise 1 with statements a–e. Which things did you already know?**

a. They **look like** friendly teddy bears but when they cry they **sound** really angry. [4]
b. It's made of plastic but it can often **feel like** the real thing. ☐
c. It doesn't **sound like** a food but it is! They **taste** really sweet and look really colourful. ☐
d. They **look** wet and slimy but when you **touch** their skin they **feel** cold and dry. ☐
e. They **smell** terrible. In fact, they **smell like** dirty old socks and they don't **taste like** fruit, but many people say they're delicious. ☐

LEARN TO LEARN
Brainstorming

Brainstorming word groups can help you make vocabulary connections.

3 **Complete each line with the words in bold in Exercise 2. Add three or more words or phrases that you associate with them.**

a. The ears: *sound, sound like, hear, listen to, music*
b. The eyes: ____________________
c. The hands: ____________________
d. The nose: ____________________
e. The tongue: ____________________

4 **Choose one group of words in Exercise 3. Say your extra words to your partner. Can they guess which group they belong to?**

5 **Complete the sentences with the correct form of the words in bold in Exercise 2.**

1. When my dad sleeps, he snores so much he *sounds like* a trumpet!
2. I tried some crocodile meat once. It __________ chicken.
3. The milk __________ bad and __________ a bit yellow, so she didn't taste it.
4. I love wearing my new winter coat. It __________ so soft and warm.
5. A It __________ a painting by Picasso.
   B No, but it is.
6. Please __________ the wall. I've just painted it.

Use it!

6 **Talk about the things in the box with the words in Exercise 2. Compare with another pair. Do you have the same descriptions?**

fast food	graffiti	mobile phones	new clothes	rap music

Explore it!

Guess the correct answer.

Which human sense is the weakest?

a sight b hearing c touch
d taste e smell

Find another interesting fact about the human senses. Write a question for your partner to answer.

READING

A magazine article

1 **Imagine you couldn't feel pain or fear. Would your life be better or worse? Why?**

4.01 2 **Read the magazine article. Which problems does it mention?**

No pain, no fear – **NO WAY!**

Everybody knows what pain feels like. It's horrible. So imagine never feeling physical pain. You cut your finger – nothing. You break your leg – no pain at all. It must be wonderful, right? Wrong, because pain is the body's way of telling the brain that there's a problem. But some people, like Amy Campbell, can't feel pain. When she was born, Amy looked like an ordinary baby, but after a few months her parents realised something was wrong and thought she had developmental problems. She would chew her tongue and bite her fingers but she never cried. By the time she was a teenager, she had broken both arms and a leg – all without feeling a thing. It also doesn't matter if the air feels hot or cold, Amy can't feel the weather. But, like any young person, she has friends, hobbies (she plays the guitar), dreams and ambitions. She just has to be very careful. You may think her life can't be easy, but Amy is optimistic about her future. She says her condition affects what she can do, but not who she is inside.

Jordy Cernik

When Jordy Cernik tells people he feels no fear, they usually think he can't be serious. Having no fear might sound like a joke but it's not. During his 20s and 30s, Jordy had to have operations to remove his adrenal glands. Some time later, he realised that these operations had had a strange effect – he couldn't feel any fear. He did a parachute jump but didn't feel scared at all. He finds rollercoasters boring. Some people imagine it must be great not to feel fear, but there are disadvantages to not having any adrenaline. Adrenaline is a natural painkiller, so Jordy now feels more pain than ordinary people. It also means he doesn't feel excited about anything. Jordy now does 'scary' challenges to raise money for charity. Doctors think he could be the only person in the world who feels no fear, but knowledge about his condition may help them understand more common problems like anxiety.

3 **Read the magazine article again. Write *T* (true), *F* (false) or *DS* (doesn't say).**

1. Amy's parents knew there was a problem when she was born. F
2. Amy wears special clothes on cold days. ___
3. Amy doesn't think her condition affects her personality. ___
4. Jordy has never been able to feel fear. ___
5. Jordy loves rollercoasters. ___
6. There are probably many people like Jordy in the world. ___
7. Doctors think studying Jordy's condition could be useful. ___

4 **Find words in the article that mean:**

1. to break food into smaller pieces with your teeth. (Amy) ________
2. the things you want to achieve. (Amy) ________
3. a chemical produced by the body. (Jordy) ________
4. a chemical or drug that stops pain. (Jordy) ________
5. the feeling of being very worried. (Jordy) ________

Voice it!

5 **Why do people enjoying doing scary things like riding on rollercoasters?**

Finished? p121 Ex 1

LANGUAGE IN ACTION

Deduction and possibility

Watch video 4.2
Why is Andy an amazing athlete? How does he know when he's near the edge of the pool?

100% certain	It [1]______ **be** wonderful.	
Possible	Having no fear [2]______ **sound like** a joke. He [4]______ **be** the only person in the world who feels no fear.	Knowledge about his condition [3]______ **help** them understand.
100% impossible	He [5]______ **be** serious.	

1 **Complete the examples in the table above. Use the magazine article on page 48 to help you.**

4.02 2 **Circle the correct words. Listen and check.**

1. This drink (must) / *can't* have lots of sugar in it. It tastes really sweet.
2. Don't touch that snake! It *might* / *can't* be poisonous.
3. This milk *must* / *can't* be really old. It smells disgusting.
4. It looks like a painting by Monet, but it *may* / *can't* be. It was painted after he died.
5. A What instrument is that? It sounds like a violin.
   B Maybe, or it *can't* / *could* be a viola.
6. This jacket *must* / *can't* be very warm in winter. It feels like a blanket!

4.03 3 **Complete the dialogue with *must*, *can't* or *might*. Listen and check.**

OMER What are you listening to? It's so loud!
BRIONY It's Beethoven. I think it's beautiful.
OMER You [1]must be joking! I thought you hated classical music.
BRIONY Well, that's because I hadn't really listened to any before. Did you know Beethoven became deaf when he was still quite young?
OMER Wow, that [2]______ be easy for anyone, but it [3]______ be absolutely terrible for a musician. You should turn it down, though. The neighbours [4]______ be home.
BRIONY They [5]______ be. The lights are off and their car's not there. Anyway, I'm sure they'd prefer Beethoven to the heavy metal you always play. They [6]______ hate that! Every time you put it on they start banging on the wall.

4 **Write sentences about this situation with the verbs and phrases in the boxes. Use *must*, *can't*, *may*, *might* or *could*.**

Marco hasn't come to school yet. He has to give a presentation with his partner, Alice, and all their notes are in Marco's locker.

be come feel have

a cold in bed late nervous soon very relaxed worried

Marco might be in bed. Alice must feel worried.

______

______

______

Use it!

5 **Look at the photos. What do you think they are?**

It could/might/can't/must be ...

It looks like (a) ...

1

2
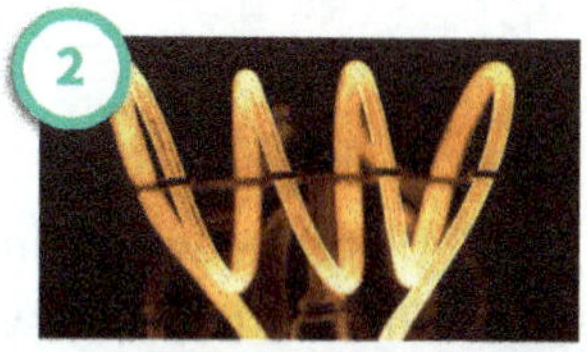

3

4

Finished? p121 Ex 2

VOCABULARY AND LISTENING

Describing texture, sound, taste, etc.

1 a sharp knife

2 a ________ umbrella

3 a ________ chameleon

4 ________ skin

5 a ________ chili

6 a ________ road

7 a ________ grapefruit

8 ________ balloons

9 a ________ skunk

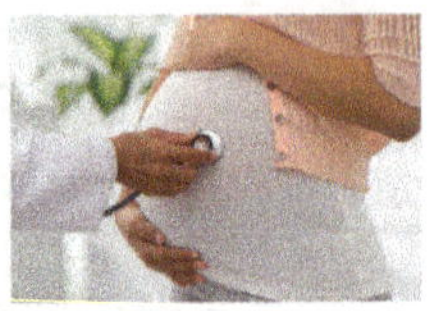

10 a ________ heartbeat

4.04 **1 Complete the photo labels with the words in the box. Listen, check and repeat.**

colourful faint rough ~~sharp~~ shiny smelly smooth sour spicy transparent

2 Complete the table with the words in Exercise 1.

Feel	Look	Smell	Sound	Taste
rough				

Use it!

3 Use the words in Exercise 1 to describe the things in the box. Can your partner guess the item?

a cat's tongue a concrete wall a curry a new coin a pencil a whisper lemons stars

It's shiny and gold. *A new coin!*

An interview

4 Foley artists create sound effects for films. What sound effects do you think these items make?

a 

b 

c 

d 

e 

a two coconut halves
b shredded newspaper and a plastic bag
c cellophane
d celery
e rice and a metal tray

I think the coconut halves could be the sound of ...

4.05 **5 Listen to the interview with James Ford, a Foley artist. Check your answers to Exercise 4.**

4.05 **6 Listen again and circle the correct words.**

1 It's important to *never* / *sometimes* have total silence in a movie.
2 The interviewer thinks the second effect is made with *newspaper* / *grass*.
3 Foley artists used to make *more* / *fewer* sounds.
4 James *made some* / *didn't make any* of the explosion sounds in his last movie.
5 To become a Foley artist, formal training is *necessary* / *unnecessary*.

LEARN TO LEARN

Using visual clues when listening

Use pictures, instructions, etc., to help you understand what you are hearing.

Voice it!

7 Do you think the job of a Foley artist will disappear in the future? Why / Why not?

LANGUAGE IN ACTION

Obligation, prohibition, necessity and advice

Watch video 4.3
What is she giving advice about?
What three things do you need to do?

1 ______ (present)	2 ______ (present)	3 ______	4 ______
They **must** sound natural.	We **need to** experiment a lot.	You **mustn't** speak loudly in the library.	We **should** listen to another one.
These days we **don't have to** do everything.	You **don't need to** have any formal training.		You **shouldn't** do that.
Do you **have to** work hard?			You **ought to** be a creative person.

Pronunciation p141

1 Complete the headings in the table above with *Obligation*, *Prohibition*, *Necessity* or *Advice*.

2 Circle the correct words.

7 TIPS FOR LOOKING AFTER YOUR EYES

1 Most of us [1]*mustn't* / *need to* (circled) use computers every day but too much screen time can be bad for your eyes.
2 You [2]*ought to* / *shouldn't* spend more than about 20 minutes looking at a screen without taking a break.
3 You [3]*should* / *shouldn't* avoid using your phone in the dark. If you want to read, you [4]*ought to* / *have to* read a book.
4 Some people [5]*don't have to* / *mustn't* wear glasses, but if you do, you [6]*should* / *ought not to* clean the lenses.
5 Buy a good pair of sunglasses: everybody [7]*needs to* / *mustn't* protect their eyes from bright sunlight.
6 Don't forget about diet either. It [8]*ought to* / *mustn't* include lots of green vegetables and fatty fish.
7 Finally, everybody [9]*doesn't have to* / *should* have an eye test once a year.

Get it right!

We don't use *must* in the past, only *had to*.

Past obligation

In the past, Foley artists [1]______ create all the effects.
I **didn't** [2]______ make those sounds.
[3]______ your parents ______ study English at school?

3 Complete the table above with the correct form of *have to*.

4 Match 1–5 with a–e. Listen and check. 4.08

1 She didn't have to study hard for the exam
2 I didn't have to wear a uniform at my last school
3 Billy didn't have to get up early this morning
4 Mia had to go to the dentist
5 I got all the answers wrong

a because it's a holiday.
b so I had to do the exercise again.
c because she had toothache.
d because she's really good at English.
e but I do at the one I go to now.

5 Complete the text with the correct form of *have to* or *should*.

Do your parents have old photos? You [1]should ask them – they might be interesting. In the past, when you took a photo, the people [2]______ stand still. They [3]______ smile but they did. The photographer [4]______ be careful because photos were expensive. Now, you [5]______ worry because you can take lots on your phone. Some people think we [6]______ take so many.

Use it!

6 Make notes and compare with a partner.

- something you had to do in the past
- something you ought to do soon

What did you have to do?

I had to visit the dentist last week!

Finished? p121 Ex 3

SPEAKING

Making guesses and giving clues

4.09 **1 Look at the picture. What are *tabi*? Listen and find out.**

4.09 **2 Complete the conversation with the phrases from the *Useful language* box. Listen and check.**

Useful language

Guess again.
Guess what it is / they are.
I guess they must be …
Perhaps it's something (+ *adjective*)
They're definitely some kind of …

AIDAN Hey, do you want to see something cool?
ZOE Sure, why not? Wow! What are those?
AIDAN They're called *tabi*. They're from Japan. [1]Guess what they are.
ZOE Well, they're [2] __________ of clothing. They look like gloves, but they can't be, can they?
AIDAN Nope. They're definitely not gloves.
ZOE They're in the shape of an 'L', so I guess [3] __________ socks.
AIDAN Bingo!
ZOE But why is the big toe separate from the other toes?
AIDAN I'm not telling you. Try and work it out yourself.
ZOE Hmm. Perhaps [4] __________ traditional. Maybe Japanese people wear rings on their big toes?
AIDAN No, that's not it. [5] __________ again.
ZOE No, I give up!
AIDAN It's so that they can wear them with sandals with straps. The strap goes between the big toe and the others.
ZOE Oh, that's a clever idea! They must be nice and warm to wear.
AIDAN I guess so. I haven't tried them on yet.

Watch video 4.4
Everyday English

Bingo! I give up! I guess so.
nice and warm/hot, etc. Sure, why not?

3 Complete the dialogues with the phrases in the *Everyday English* box.

1 A Shall we watch a movie? B __________
2 It's __________ today. Let's have a picnic!
3 A Is the answer 23? B __________
4 A Chinese must be hard to learn. B __________
5 A One more guess? B No – __________

PLAN

4 Write about something from your country that might be new or strange to a foreigner, for example a food or an item of clothing. How would you describe it?

____

____

SPEAK

5 Practise describing something from your country to your partner. Remember to use modals, vocabulary from this unit and phrases from the *Useful language* and *Everyday English* boxes.

CHECK

6 Work with another pair. Listen to their conversation and complete the notes.

What did you hear about? __________________

____

How was it described? __________________

____

WRITING
An encyclopaedia entry

1 **Look at the pictures. What is attached to the man's head? Read the encyclopaedia entry and find out.**

2 **Match titles a–e with paragraphs 1–5.**

a Artwork
b Other information
c Introduction
d Name and date of birth
e Life

1 ☐ Neil Harbisson, 27 July 1984

2 ☐ Neil Harbisson is known as the world's first cyborg artist. He has been colour blind since birth and has a special antenna connected to his skull that lets him 'hear' colours as different vibrations in his head.

3 ☐ Neil was born in Belfast in 1984 and grew up in Barcelona. At the age of 16, he started to make black and white art. In 2004, scientists developed his special camera and attached it to his head. With the camera, Neil can 'hear' 360 colours, including some which are invisible to the human eye. In 2004, when he had to get a new passport, the UK passport office said no at first because he didn't look like a human. However, they finally accepted his application. He must be the only official cyborg in the world.

4 ☐ Neil now makes colourful art, including 'sound portraits' of famous people and geometric paintings. He has had exhibitions all around the world.

5 ☐ According to Neil, all human skin sounds orange.

3 **Are the sentences *T* (true) or *F* (false)?**

1 Neil has always lived in the same place. ___
2 Neil doesn't always wear his antenna. ___
3 Neil can experience colours that ordinary humans can't see. ___
4 Neil couldn't get a new British passport. ___
5 People in many countries have seen Neil's art. ___

4 **Complete the sentences with the phrases from the *Useful language* box.**

1 Stefani Joanne Angelina Germanotta ________________ Lady Gaga.
2 She ________________ 28 March 1986 ________________ New York City.
3 ________________ four she began to learn to play the piano.
4 She makes energetic pop music, ________________ songs like *Bad Romance* and *Alejandro*.
5 ________________ Lady Gaga, you can teach yourself art.

Useful language

According to …	… is known as …
At the age of …	… was born on …
including …	and grew up in …

Write an encyclopaedia entry.

PLAN

5 **These artists all have a physical difference. Choose one and make notes about them.**

photographer Roesie Percy
chef Adam Cole
rapper Sean Forbes

name and date of birth
their life
their artwork

WRITE

6 **Write your encyclopaedia entry. Remember to include five paragraphs, modal verbs, vocabulary from this unit and phrases from the *Useful language* box.**

CHECK

7 **Do you …**

- include information about the person's life?
- include information about the person's artwork?

Finished? p121 Ex 4

THE SCIENCE PROJECT

An infographic on animal senses

1 **Work in pairs. Can you answer the questions?**

1. Which continents do elephants live in?
2. How do they know where they are going?
3. How strong is their trunk (their long nose)?
4. What do they use their ears for?

2 **Read the infographic and check your answers to Exercise 1.**

How to research

3 **Which of these things should you do when you research? Tick the correct answers.**

1. Decide the main information you want before doing research. ✓
2. Use questions in search engines, e.g. *How well can elephants see?* ☐
3. Read articles from start to finish. ☐
4. Read the contents list of articles or the titles of sections and then decide what you need to read. ☐
5. Make sure the information is fact and not opinion. ☐
6. Only check information on one site. ☐
7. Take notes as you read. ☐

Elephants and

Elephants' eyes are on the side of their head and have three eyelids, one above the eye, one below, like humans, and an almost transparent one they use to keep dust, dirt and water out. However, their eyes aren't very strong. They normally use their trunks to know where they are going. In fact, the leader of a group of elephants is sometimes blind.

Elephants can hear extremely well because they have big ears. They can hear faint sounds, including the calls of elephants up to 1.5 km away. Their ears are about $^{1}/_{6}$ of the size of their bodies. They also use them to keep cool.

Elephants have to move their trunk around and smell the air all the time in order to find water, so they have an excellent sense of smell. They can detect water up to 12 km away.

Elephants use their rough trunks to explore the environment and care for their young. They also use it to fight. The trunk can lift objects that weigh up to 250 kg. They can also sense tiny vibrations in the ground with their feet. Scientists think this must be the reason why many survived the Asian Tsunami of 2004. They felt the vibrations of the earthquake and moved to higher ground.

OWN IT!

their **amazing** senses

- Two species: African and Asian
- Males: 2,700 to 6,300 kg
- Females: 1,800 to 3,600 kg
- Lifespan: approx. 65 years
- 100,000 muscles in the trunk

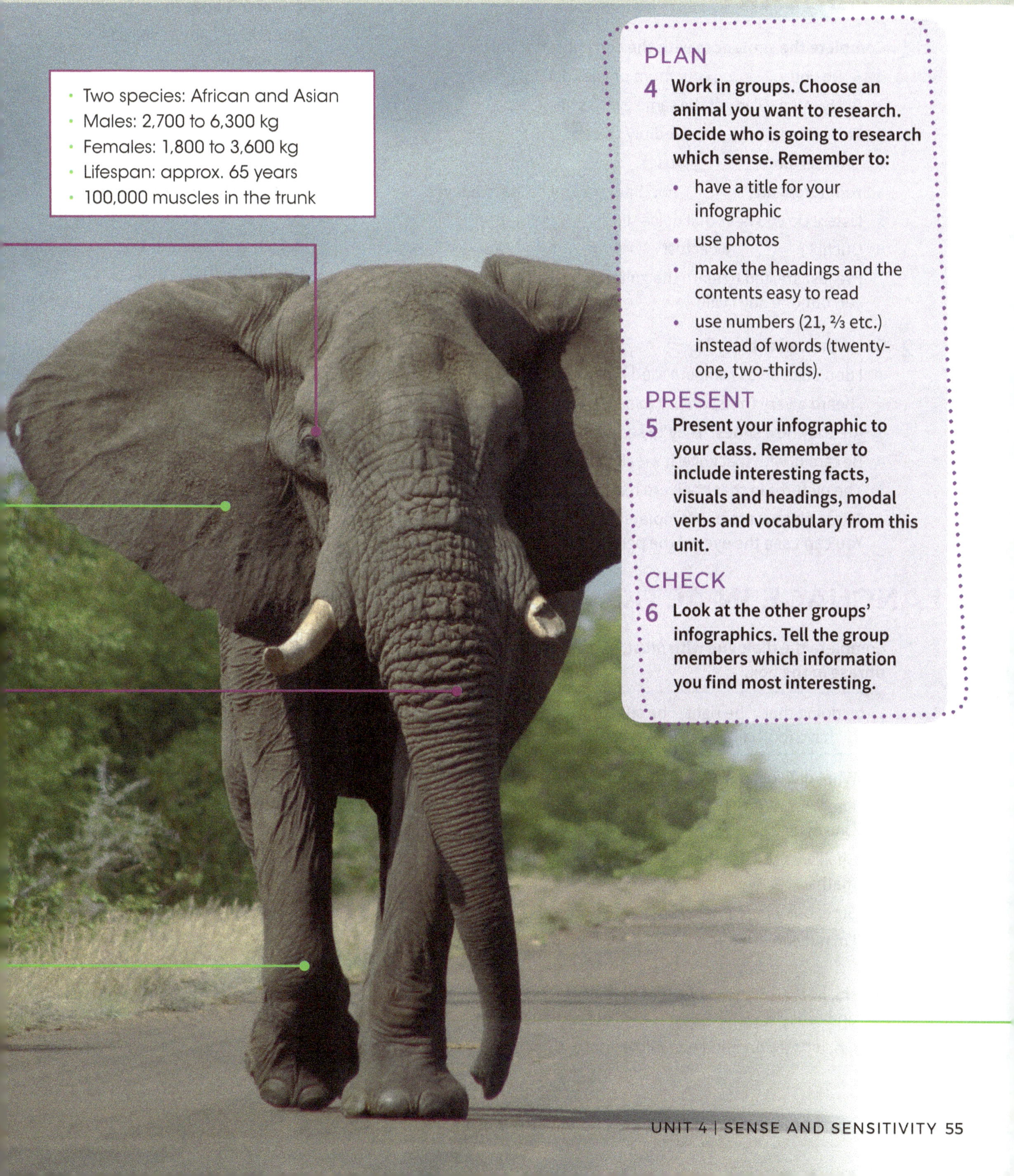

PLAN

4 **Work in groups. Choose an animal you want to research. Decide who is going to research which sense. Remember to:**

- have a title for your infographic
- use photos
- make the headings and the contents easy to read
- use numbers (21, ⅔ etc.) instead of words (twenty-one, two-thirds).

PRESENT

5 **Present your infographic to your class. Remember to include interesting facts, visuals and headings, modal verbs and vocabulary from this unit.**

CHECK

6 **Look at the other groups' infographics. Tell the group members which information you find most interesting.**

4 REVIEW

VOCABULARY

1 Complete the sentences with the correct sense verb.

1 A Do you ________ your mum or your dad?
B My mum – I've got the same eyes as her.
2 This coffee ________ incredibly sweet.
3 Your perfume ________ roses.
4 Your forehead ________ hot, Sam. You might have a fever.
5 Listen! Do you hear that noise? It ________ a mouse.
6 Ouch! I ________ a cactus!
7 I've just started to learn the guitar. I ________ very good yet, but one day I will.

2 Circle the correct words.

1 I don't like *spicy* / *smooth* food much – it burns my mouth.
2 I heard a very *transparent* / *faint* sound in the distance.
3 Are they new shoes? They're so *smelly* / *shiny* – I love them!
4 Be careful with that knife! It's really *sharp* / *faint*.
5 The pictures in that book are really *sour* / *colourful*.
6 These glasses are not completely *smelly* / *transparent*. You can't see the eyes of the person wearing them.

LANGUAGE IN ACTION

3 Complete the dialogue with *must*, *might* or *can't* and a phrase in the box.

be doing that · be right · be studying · be wrong · have football practice · know the answer

A What did you answer for question 10? I put 65.5.
B I put 75.3. We [1] ________________ both ________________. One of us [2] ________________.
A Shall we ask Tim? He [3] ________________. He's good at maths.
B Sure, but where is he?
A I'm not sure. He [4] ________________ in the library or he [5] ________________.
B No, he [6] ________________. Football practice is on Tuesday and today is Wednesday.
A OK, let's try and find him in the library then.

4 Match 1–5 with a–e. Complete the sentences with *have*/*has to*, *don't*/*doesn't have to*, *must*/*mustn't* or *had to*/*didn't have to*.

1 Eric got up early yesterday because he ________ ☐
2 This seat is reserved for old people so you ________ ☐
3 I've got lots to do tomorrow so I really ________ ☐
4 My friend had his car so we ________ ☐
5 Before visitors enter the exhibition, they ________ ☐

a sit there.
b start work at 7 am.
c take the bus.
d put their bags in a locker.
e go to bed soon.

Self-assessment

I can use verbs to talk about senses.	☹	😐	☺
I can use adjectives to describe texture, sound, taste, etc.	☹	😐	☺
I can use modals of deduction and possibility.	☹	😐	☺
I can use modals of obligation, prohibition, necessity and advice.	☹	😐	☺

LEARN TO LEARN

LEARN TO … PLAN YOUR HOMEWORK

When you have a lot of homework to do, it's important to decide what order to do it in and when to do it.

1 Ask and answer questions 1–4 in the leaflet with a partner. Are your answers similar or different?

Feeling stressed about homework?

With our useful advice, you don't need to panic!

How often have you …

1 forgotten what you had to do for homework?
2 handed in a piece of homework late because you didn't start it until too late?
3 not started until you're too tired?
4 done the quick or easy homework first and then not had time for more difficult things?

If you answered 'often' or 'always', then you really need our help!

a Decide when you need to start your homework and give yourself enough time.
b When you ought to start but don't want to, tell yourself, 'I'll just do five minutes'. Once you start, it's easy to continue.
c You should think about how difficult a piece of homework is or how much time it needs.
d When you get your homework, write it down immediately and always in the same place.

Now use our homework planner and start planning!

2 Match advice a–d with the problems in questions 1–4.

1 ________ 2 ________ 3 ________ 4 ________

3 Helen is planning her homework. What should she do first and last on Saturday? Why?

Homework Planner **Student's name:** Helen

1 What is the subject and homework task?	2 When do I have to hand the homework in?	3 From 1–5, how easy/difficult is it? 1= very easy, 5= very difficult	4 How much time do I need to do it?	5 What day am I going to do it?	6 On each day, what am I going to do first, second etc.?
Maths, p38 Exercises 6–9	Monday	3	45 minutes	Saturday	
History, essay	Monday	5	1 1/2 hours	Saturday	
Science, p67 Exercises 3 and 4	Monday	4	1 hour	Saturday	
Geography, project	Wednesday	4	2 1/2 hours	Sunday	

OWN IT!

4 Think about the homework you have to do this week. Use the homework planner to plan it.

1 FINISHED?

1 Put the letters in order to make words to describe clothes and shoes.

1 E O L F W R Y — flowery

2 P S O D T E T ______

3 R I S T E D P ______

4 H I T G T ______

5 H D C E C K E ______

6 A L T F ______

7 E I H E H L E H D G ______

8 V E O N E L S E G D L ______

2 Match the texts with photos a–d.

1 I've just had a totally amazing time! I've been looking at all sorts of interesting animals, with lots of fantastic colours. I haven't done anything like this before, but I'd like to do it again. I've told all my friends, and they want to do it with me next time. ______

2 We've just come back, and we've spent all our money. The good news is now I've got lots of really good clothes, so I don't need to do anything like this again for a long time! ______

3 I've been outside all day, and now I'm feeling pretty tired. I've being doing this since I was very young, and one day, I want to train other people to do the same as me. ______

4 I've had a rather bad experience. I haven't tasted anything so bad for a long time. And since I had it, I've been feeling quite ill. My stomach has been hurting for ages. I'm never going back there, and I'm going to tell all my friends about it!

a 

b 

c 

d 

3 Complete the modifiers with vowels. Make sentences with the modifiers and the words in the box about you.

amazed	better	confused	good at
happier	happy	more interesting	
shocked	slow	slower	taller

1 absolutely
2 _xtr_m_ly
3 r__lly
4 t_t_lly
5 f__rly
6 pr_tty
7 q__t_
8 r_th_r
9 _ l_t
10 _ l_ttl_
11 _ b_t

4 Put the letters in order to make verbs to describe clothes and shoes. Use the letters in the circles to make an expression. Write the mystery expression.

1 WIGOHT — GO WITH
2 MTCAH — □□□□□
3 TIF — □□□
4 WERTAUO — □□□□ □□□
5 UTSI — □□□□
6 HAPNUG — □□□□ □□
7 LOFD — □□□□
8 POUD — □□ □□
9 NODU — □□□□

Mystery expression: □□ □□□ □□ □□□□□□□

2 FINISHED?

1 **Read the clues and complete the crossword.**

Across

3 I had to do … my phone for a week, because it was broken.
5 Last week, I went … to my old primary school to visit my teacher.
6 I feel bad. I hope I don't … up getting ill.
7 I've … up for piano lessons.

Down

1 I … through a difficult time when I started my new school, but now everything's OK.
2 Sara … out of her old flat, and went to live in a new one.
4 I … down three party invitations last month because I was so busy.

2 **Compare the pictures. How many sentences can you write about Stuart's life in the past with *used to, didn't use to* and *would*? Use your imagination!**

When Stuart was a student, he used to live in a flat.

3 **What films had you seen by the time you were ten? Write as many as possible in two minutes.**

4 **Find words in the sentences that rhyme with parts of objects. Change them so the sentences make sense.**

1 Put the ~~kid~~ back or the pen will dry. lid
2 I've broken the sandal on my bag. ______
3 My computer needs a hug. ______
4 The Swiss play on that phone is really bright. ______
5 Don't get the camera pens dirty. ______
6 The map of my bag hurts my shoulder. It's too tight. ______

3 FINISHED?

1 Match the squares to make cooking verbs.

ro	ch	over	gri	sea	pe	sli	fr	ba	spre	gra	he
y	son	te	ke	ll	at	ad	ast	cook	ce	el	op

2 Use the code to write the questions. Answer them so they are true for you.

A = ✑	B = ☞	C = ■	D = ✘	E = ✈
F = ●	G = ❍	H = ✧	I = ❄	J = ✍
K = ✉	L = ✎	M = ✢	N = ✪	O = ✓
P = ☎	Q = ✾	R = ☮	S = ❑	T = ✐
U = ✳	V = ✶	W = ✂	X = ✆	Y = ✻

1 ✘✓❄✪❍ ✐✧❄❑ ✈✶✈✪❄✪❍
What are you ______________________________?
____

2 ❍✓❄✪❍ ✐✓ ✘✓ ✪✈✆✐ ❑✳✢✢✈☮
What are you ______________________________?
____

3 ☎✈✓☎✎✈ ✂❄✎✎ ✐☮✑✶✈✎ ❄✪ ✐✧✈ ●✳✐✳☮✈
How do you think ______________________________?
____

4 ✂✈✑✐✧✈☮ ❍✓❄✪❍ ✐✓ ☞✈ ✎❄✉✈ ✐✓✢✓☮☮✓✂
What's the ______________________________?
____

3 Make sentences with the verbs in the box and the future continuous and future perfect.

chat to friends do homework
do sport have dinner
listen to music sleep

At 5 pm I will / won't be …
At 7 pm …
At 11 pm …
By midnight I will / won't have …

____
____
____
____
____
____
____

4 Circle nine more quantities.

H	A	N	D	F	U	L	T	G	F	D
V	Y	D	B	E	H	E	E	D	G	X
S	P	R	I	N	K	L	E	C	C	O
L	K	J	K	C	O	I	C	K	E	W
E	A	S	A	W	U	S	V	I	A	E
E	J	P	D	F	B	P	I	E	C	E
P	Q	O	F	V	S	L	L	C	H	J
O	I	O	V	C	K	A	W	E	U	K
P	J	N	E	D	A	S	I	O	N	R
C	H	F	C	W	Y	H	N	D	K	N
Q	R	U	J	H	Q	B	G	G	R	T
W	S	L	I	C	E	H	T	I	O	M

4 FINISHED?

1 Can you work out these riddles?

1 Sometimes they look like faces, sometimes they look like animals. They're always changing shape. Grey ones usually disappear after the rain.

____

2 It looks like a tear and it tastes a bit like an apple. It sounds the same as two things of the same size that are used together.

____

3 Mine sounds like a bird. Mary's latest one sounds like a famous pop song. We don't know what Dave's sounds like because he always has his mobile on silent.

____

2 Look at the dots. Write four things you think it could be. Join the dots to see if you are right.

It could/might be a ball ...

____

____

____

____

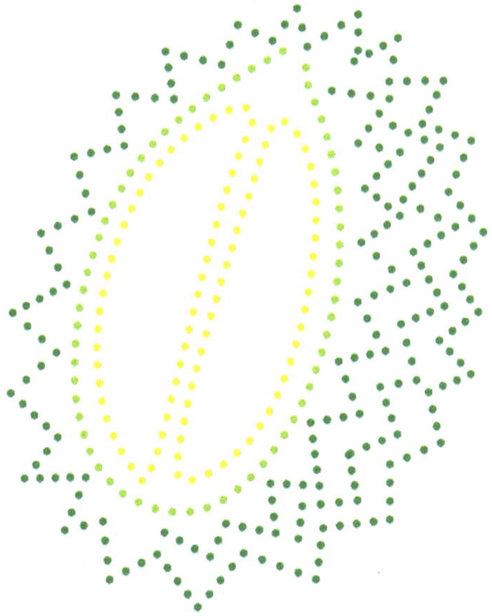

3 Imagine you do an unusual job. Write as many of these as possible in three minutes.

- things you had to do to get your job

- things you have to do every day in your job.

Show your list to a partner. Can they guess the job?

4 Circle nine more adjectives.

R	U	Z	D	H	S	W	I	D	D	T	L
C	O	L	M	S	H	A	R	P	F	R	U
H	G	U	J	T	I	C	Y	L	S	A	F
N	T	X	G	H	N	A	B	U	M	V	R
S	V	O	D	H	Y	L	Q	S	E	U	U
M	K	L	O	D	E	F	E	B	L	H	O
A	I	P	R	M	K	M	U	Z	L	E	L
O	F	H	Z	G	S	P	I	C	Y	F	O
T	A	S	O	U	R	O	W	J	A	C	C
H	D	R	M	V	P	A	S	I	L	J	E
T	N	E	R	A	P	S	N	A	R	T	H
O	S	Q	U	G	A	T	V	Z	N	I	F

STARTER VOCABULARY BANK

Travel

accommodation

backpacking

holiday resort

sightseeing

tourist attraction

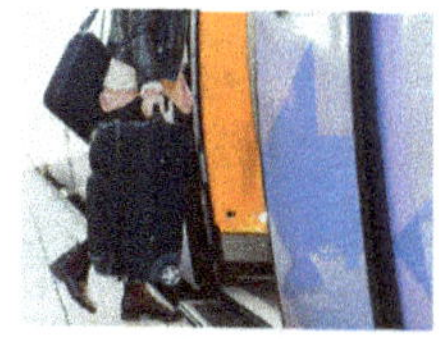
trip

Music and theatre

audience lines	part rehearsal	scene show

1 Are the sentences true or false?

	True	False
1 An audience is all the actors in a play.	☐	☐
2 A holiday resort is a shop where you go to book a holiday.	☐	☐
3 The lines in a play are the words the actors speak.	☐	☐
4 Your accommodation is the plane, boat, etc. that takes you to your holiday.	☐	☐
5 Actors have rehearsals to practise their performance.	☐	☐

Ways of communicating

describe greet	post shake hands	shout smile	translate wave	whisper

2 Circle the correct words.

1 At the beginning of the trip, we were *posted* / *greeted* / *waved* by our tour guide.
2 I think he enjoyed the show because he was *shouting* / *waving* / *smiling*.
3 Alfonso will *describe* / *translate* / *whisper* all the tourist attractions we are going to see.
4 She plays the part of an angry teacher who *shouts* / *posts* / *smiles* at her students a lot.
5 In the first scene, two actors meet and *translate* / *shake hands* / *describe*.

LEARN TO LEARN

Personalising vocabulary

Writing personalised sentences helps you to learn new words.

3 Choose four verbs from the list above and write sentences that are true for you. Then tell your partner.

1 ____________________
2 ____________________
3 ____________________
4 ____________________

Our teacher greets us every morning.

1 VOCABULARY BANK

Describing clothes and shoes

baggy

checked

cotton

denim

flat

flowery

high-heeled

long-sleeved

plain

spotted

striped

tight

1 Is the adjective order correct or incorrect? Circle the correct answer.

1 We have to wear leather flat shoes. *Correct / Incorrect*
2 Paul was wearing a red baggy T-shirt. *Correct / Incorrect*
3 Laura bought a flowery cotton blouse. *Correct / Incorrect*
4 I'd like a denim black jacket. *Correct / Incorrect*
5 The singer wore tight striped trousers. *Correct / Incorrect*

Verbs related to clothes and shoes

do up fit fold	go out of fashion go with	hang up match suit	undo wear out

2 Circle the correct words.

1 I can't wear this spotted scarf. It doesn't *hang up / go with / fold* my coat.
2 This dress is a bit tight. It doesn't *match / undo / fit* me any more.
3 I've had this sweater for years. It never seems to *wear out / suit me / undo me*.
4 Don't leave your jacket on the floor. *Hang it up / Do it up / Wear it out* in your wardrobe.
5 You look great in that checked shirt. It really *goes out of fashion / suits you / goes with you*.

LEARN TO LEARN

Categorising

Recording new words in categories helps you to remember their meaning.

3 Put the clothes verbs above in the correct categories. Compare with a partner.

Putting clothes away	hang up
Ways of saying that clothes look good	
Reasons not to wear clothes	
Putting on and taking off clothes	

2 VOCABULARY BANK

Phrasal verbs: changes

do without	go back	look forward to	move to	sign up	turn down
end up	go through	move out	settle down	try out	turn out

1 Complete the statements with a phrasal verb from the list. Put them in order from most true for you (1) to least true for you (5). Compare with a partner.

1 I would love to ________ New York. ________
2 I never ________ party invitations. ________
3 I always ________ my English classes. ________
4 I like to ________ new video games with my friends. ________
5 I would like to ________ in one place for my whole life. ________

Parts of objects

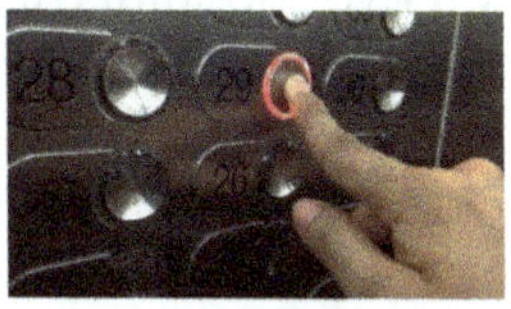
button

cable

cover

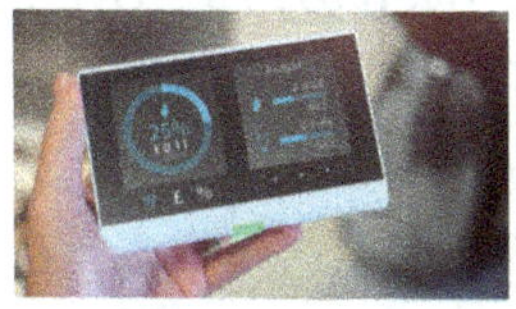
display

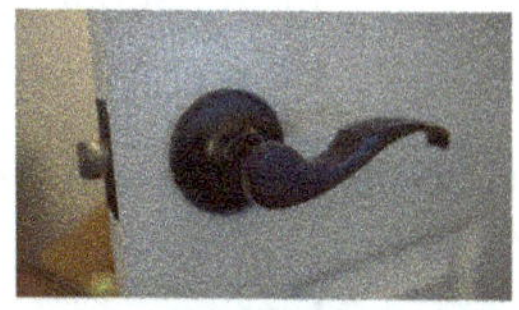
handle

key

lens

lid

plug

strap

2 Use the clues to find the mystery word. Write your own clue for the mystery word.

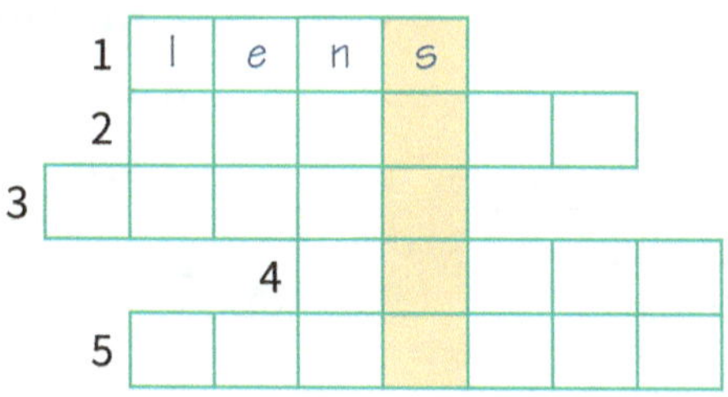

1 I'm made of glass. You look through me.
2 I am round. You press me to make a lift come.
3 I'm made of paper. I go on books to protect them.
4 I am long and thin. I bring electricity to objects.
5 I show information, for example the time.

Mystery word: ________ Your clue: ____________________

LEARN TO LEARN

Visualising words in different situations

Visualising words in different situations helps you to remember them.

3 Where would you find these parts (1–4)? Use the objects from the box. Some may have more than one part. Then choose two more parts from the list above and think of objects that have them.

keyboard	TV	jam jar	laptop	vacuum cleaner	saucepan	door	shoe box

1 key ________ 2 handle ________ 3 lid ________ 4 plug ________

3 VOCABULARY BANK

Cooking verbs

bake

chop

fry

grate

grill

heat

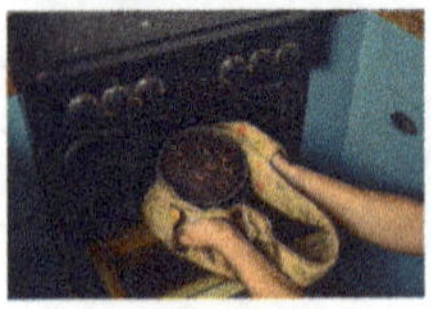
overcook

peel

roast

season

slice

spread

1 Put the verbs in the correct place so that this potato recipe makes sense.

First, [1]*season* the oven to 220°. [2]*Overcook* the potatoes and [3]*peel* them into large pieces. Add two spoonfuls of oil and [4]*heat* with some salt and pepper. [5]*Chop* the potatoes for 45 minutes, but be careful not to [6]*roast* them!

1 heat 2 ________ 3 ________ 4 ________ 5 ________ 6 ________

Quantities

a chunk of a cup of	a handful of a packet of	a piece of a pinch of	a slice of a splash of	a spoonful of a sprinkle of

2 Match 1–5 with a–e.

1 This sauce isn't sweet enough. I'm going to add a spoonful of ________
2 I'm cooking tonight. We're having a lovely piece of ________
3 Grill the fish with a pinch of ________
4 I'm going to fry the potatoes with a splash of ________
5 The soup will be delicious because she's putting in a handful of ________

a sugar.
b oil.
c fresh herbs.
d beef.
e salt.

LEARN TO LEARN

Word partners

When you learn new words, try to learn words that go with them so that you can use them in natural contexts.

3 Choose four quantities and think of three food items to go with each one. Compare with a partner.

1 ____________________
2 ____________________
3 ____________________
4 ____________________

a chunk of cheese, meat, potato.

4 VOCABULARY BANK

The five senses

feel	look	smell	sound	taste	touch
feel like	look like	smell like	sound like	taste like	

1 **Complete the sentences with the words in the box.**

delicious stone a train fresh bread icy

1 Has someone been baking? It smells like __________ in here.
2 It's actually wood, but it's so cold, it feels like __________ .
3 I don't know what's in this dish, but it tastes __________ .
4 I heard a loud noise. It sounded a bit like __________ .
5 Be careful when you go outside. The pavement looks __________ .

Describing texture, sound, taste, etc.

colourful

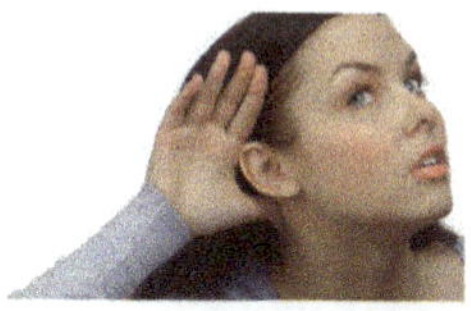
faint

rough

sharp

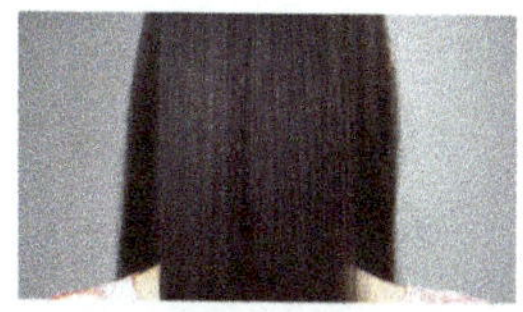
shiny

smelly

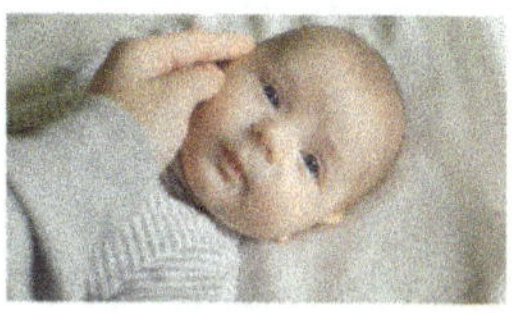
smooth

sour

spicy

transparent

2 **Match 1–5 with a–e.**

1 You've worn that shirt for three days. ________
2 Be careful with that knife. ________
3 The noise can't be coming from this room. ________
4 Antonio washed his car yesterday. ________
5 I think it must be lemon juice. ________

a It tastes rather sour.
b It's too faint.
c It must be a bit smelly.
d It looks very sharp.
e That's why it's so shiny.

LEARN TO LEARN

Brainstorming

Brainstorming word groups can help you make vocabulary connections.

3 **Choose three of the words from the list above and brainstorm connected words with your partner.**

1 ______________________________
2 ______________________________
3 ______________________________

shiny: shoes, hair, gold, metal, glass, car, clean.

2 HISTORY

1 Look at the title and picture and discuss the questions.

1 When do you think this picture was taken?

2 Where are the people and what are they doing?

2 Read the text. Check your answer to question 2 in Exercise 1. 2.14

STARTING AGAIN

Between 1880 and 1910, 17 million Europeans made the decision to move to the United States and start a new life. Many of them never went back to their country of birth. This was part of what is known as the Great Atlantic **Migration**. It started in the 1840s and it is the largest migration in history.

For many people, it was the first time they had ever left their hometown. The two-week journey was very unpleasant, and on larger ships up to 2,000 people were **crammed** into the lower **decks**. It was dark, there was little fresh water, and the air was **rancid**. So why choose to go through such a difficult experience?

One major reason was hunger. For example, in Ireland in the 1840s, people used to depend on potatoes for food. When the potato crop failed for three years in a row, there was not enough to eat and around one million people died. After this, half of the Irish population decided to move to the United States. They were nervous about the journey, but they looked forward to a better life.

> I am exceedingly well pleased at coming to this land of plenty.

Letter from an Irish immigrant to The Times, *London, 1850*

Immigrants from all over Europe had their own story to tell. Although they had never experienced life in the United States before, they arrived ready to **settle** in a new culture. Immigrants helped build the United States into the country it is today. Like all migrations, the Great Atlantic Migration is the story of people making difficult decisions for the chance to start again.

3 Read the text again. Write *T* (true), *F* (false) or *DS* (doesn't say).

1 Most immigrants to the United States eventually returned to their country of birth. ___

2 There wasn't much room on board the ships. ___

3 Poverty was a major reason for migration. ___

4 Irish immigrants felt hopeful about their future. ___

5 Immigrants from all over Europe moved for the same reasons as the Irish. ___

6 They made a positive contribution to American society. ___

4 Discuss other possible causes of migration throughout history and up to the present day.

5 Complete the definitions with the words in bold in the text.

1 ________ (n) the act of moving from one place to another

2 ________ (n) the floors of a ship

3 ________ (v) to make a home

4 ________ (v) to be filled with something so there is no more room

5 ________ (adj) having a very bad smell (or taste)

Explore it!

Guess the correct answer.

How many people live in a country different to the one they were born in?

a over 50 million

b over 150 million

c over 250 million

Find another interesting fact about migration. Write a question for your partner to answer.

Echolocation

Imagine you are walking with a torch through a forest at night. Suddenly, the light goes out and you cannot see a thing. You feel a branch brush your face and smell the leaves on the trees. You need to go home, but how can you find your way?

If you were a bat, you would use echolocation. Echolocation is a technique used by some animals to move around in the dark. It helps them identify friends and enemies and 'see' where they are going. Here are two examples of how animals use it.

Bats

To hunt for insects in the dark, bats make a **high-pitched** call as they fly, then listen for the returning **echo**. They calculate how far away something is by how long it takes the echo to return. A bat can **detect** an insect in the dark from a distance of five metres!

Dolphins

To identify objects in deep, dark waters, dolphins produce high-frequency **clicks**. These create sound waves that **bounce back** as echoes. This information helps dolphins work out the distance, direction of travel, speed and size of things.

But you don't have to be a bat or a dolphin to echolocate. You might be surprised to learn that some humans can echolocate too. One such person is Daniel Kish. Daniel is completely blind, so he gets information about what is around him by clicking his tongue and listening to the echo. This technique allows him to safely ride a bike or go hiking in the wild. He also trains other blind people to echolocate. Amazing, isn't it?

1 Discuss the questions.

1. What special skills do the animals in the pictures have?
2. What do they use these skills for?

4.10 **2 Read the article. Check your answers to Exercise 1.**

3 Complete the table with information from the article.

	Sound	How it helps
Bat	1	4
Dolphin	2	5
Daniel Kish	3	6

4 Complete the text with the words in bold in the article.

Whales, like dolphins, produce [1]________ to work out an object's distance, direction, speed and size. These sounds can be low- or [2]________. The sounds hit an object and [3]________ to the whale's throat. The time it takes the [4]________ of these sounds to return to the whale helps the animal to [5]________, or sense, what is around it.

Explore it!

Guess the correct answer.

Some bats have a scream as loud as a …

a. jet engine 30 metres away.
b. very loud opera singer.
c. machine that breaks rocks.

Find another interesting fact about bats, whales or echolocation. Write a question for your partner to answer.

PRONUNCIATION

UNIT 1

The letters *ea*

1.08 **1 Listen and repeat.**

1 /eə/ wear 2 /e/ bread 3 /iː/ meat 4 /eɪ/ steak

2 Put the words in the correct column according to the pronunciation of the letters *ea*.

break clean great head heaven
peach ~~pear~~ please weather

/eə/	/e/	/iː/	/eɪ/
pear			

1.09 **3 Listen, check and repeat.**

UNIT 2

used to

2.04 **1 Listen and repeat.**

1 He used to go out with his friends every weekend.
2 Did you use to like cats when you were younger?

2.05 **2 Listen to the sentences. Are the words in bold pronounced the same in each sentence?**

1 She **used a** friend's phone to call her parents.
2 She **used to** have her mum's phone.

2.06 **3 Listen and write the sentences.**

1 ______
2 ______
3 ______
4 ______

4 Practise saying the sentences.

1 She used to play football after school.
2 My dad used to listen to classical music.
3 Did you use to live here?

2.07 **5 Listen and check.**

UNIT 3

The letters *ch*

3.03 **1 Listen and repeat.**

1 /ʃ/ machine 2 /tʃ/ cheese 3 /k/ school

2 Put the words in the correct column according to the pronunciation of the letters *ch*

check chemistry chorus
headache mechanic ~~moustache~~
parachute reach search touch

/ʃ/	/tʃ/	/k/
moustache		

3.04 **3 Listen, check and repeat.**

UNIT 4

Weak form of *to*

4.06 **1 Listen and repeat.**

1 He has to work late tonight.
2 I need to buy new shoes.
3 We ought to take an umbrella.

4.07 **2 Listen and underline the stressed words.**

1 I'd like to know what time the film starts.
2 We have to leave early tomorrow.
3 You ought to study more for your exams.
4 Do you need to make a phone call?

4.07 **3 Listen, check and repeat.**

4 Practise saying the sentences with the correct pronunciation of *to*.

1 Do you think we ought to tell him?
2 Erin needs to go food shopping.
3 I'd like to go to the party but my mum says I have to stay home.

OWN IT! 4

B1 Preliminary test content in *Own It!* Level 4 has been checked by Cambridge Assessment English for accuracy and level.

WORKBOOK

Eoin Higgins and Philip Wood

CAMBRIDGE UNIVERSITY PRESS

CONTENTS

Starter Unit Welcome! p4

Unit 1 Trendsetters p8

Unit 2 Changes p16

Unit 3 Food for thought p24

Unit 4 Sense and sensitivity p32

Exam tips and practice p80

Language reference and practice p86

Language bank p106

Irregular verbs p111

STARTER

WELCOME!

VOCABULARY AND READING

Travel

1 ☆ **Match the words with the definitions.**

accommodation backpacking
holiday resort sightseeing
tourist attractions ~~trip~~

1 a journey where you visit a place for a short time and then come back again ___trip___
2 visiting places that are interesting because they are historical, famous, etc. ______
3 travelling or walking, carrying your things in a bag on your back ______
4 monuments or places that people on holiday like to visit ______
5 a town or place where people go on holiday, very often next to the sea ______
6 a place where you live or stay ______

2 ☆ **Complete the sentences so they are true for you. (See the *Learn to learn* tip in the Student's Book, p4.)**

1 ______ is a famous tourist attraction in my country.
2 For our accommodation on our last holiday, we stayed in ______ .
3 ______ is a popular holiday resort in my country.
4 The last trip I went on was to ______ .
5 In my opinion, going backpacking is a ______ way to spend your holiday.
6 I would like to go sightseeing in ______ .

Music and theatre

3 ☆☆ **Complete the text. The first letter of each word is given.**

I was quite surprised when Ms Bayliss gave me the biggest [1]p___art___ in the school musical. It wasn't easy to learn all my [2]l______ but, after several [3]r______ , I knew them perfectly. I was nervous on the day of the [4]s______ because all my family were in the [5]a______ . But everything went well, and after the final [6]s______ , everyone stood up and clapped!

An interview

4 ☆ **Read the interview. What did Jed do on holiday? Choose the correct photo.**

a  ☐

b  ☐

MIA So, where did you go on holiday, Jed?
JED Italy – it was a fantastic trip!
MIA Did you stay at a holiday resort?
JED No, it was a hotel. We did a lot of sightseeing. We went to some famous tourist attractions, like the Colosseum in Rome. It was amazing!
MIA So, what was the best part of your trip?
JED Oh, that was when we saw an opera: The Barber of Seville in the *Teatro Argentina* – it's almost three hundred years old! It's an amazing place – so beautiful!
MIA But wasn't the opera in Italian?
JED Yes, it was, and most of the audience was Italian, but there were subtitles.

5 ☆☆ **Read the interview again and answer the questions.**

1 Where did Jed stay?
______
2 What did Jed think of the Colosseum?
______
3 What did Jed do in Rome?
______
4 Why could Jed understand the opera?
______

LANGUAGE IN ACTION AND VOCABULARY

Present and past simple and continuous

1 **Write the sentences in the past.**

1 Dan is reading the paper.
   Dan was reading the paper.
2 They aren't listening to music.
   ____
3 Am I making a lot of noise?
   ____
4 Beth usually plays football on Saturday.
   ____
5 They don't live in a flat.
   ____
6 Does Michael eat meat?
   ____

2 **Complete the conversation with the verbs in the box in the correct tense.**

~~be~~ do enjoy have help visit

A How [1] ___was___ your trip to Paris?
B Great, thanks! I [2] __________ it a lot!
A What [3] __________ (you) __________ there?
B We [4] __________ lots of tourist attractions!
A You're so lucky! While you [5] __________ a great time in Paris, I [6] __________ my dad to paint the house!

3 **Answer the questions with true information.**

1 What did you do last weekend?
   ____
2 What were you doing at nine o'clock last night?
   ____
3 What does your dad do?
   ____
4 What's your mum probably doing at the moment?
   ____

Ways of communicating

4 **Circle eight more communication verbs in the word snake.**

postshoutwhisperdescribesmiletranslateshakehandsgreetwave

5 **Complete the table with the verbs from Exercise 4. Some verbs go in both columns.**

You can use your hands to do this	You can use your mouth to do this
post	5 __________
1 __________	6 __________
2 __________	7 __________
3 __________	8 __________
4 __________	9 __________
	10 __________

6 **Complete the sentences with the verbs from Exercise 4.**

1 Do you know anyone who can ___translate___ from English into Chinese?
2 Could you __________ this letter for me?
3 Please don't __________ ! I can hear you!
4 How would you __________ your personality?
5 When you __________ , you feel happier.
6 If you don't know the answer when the teacher asks you, I'll __________ it to you very quietly.
7 When film stars arrive at the Oscars, they often __________ to the crowd.
8 When I have my interview tomorrow, how should I __________ the person who is interviewing me? Should I __________ with them?

LISTENING AND LANGUAGE IN ACTION

A conversation

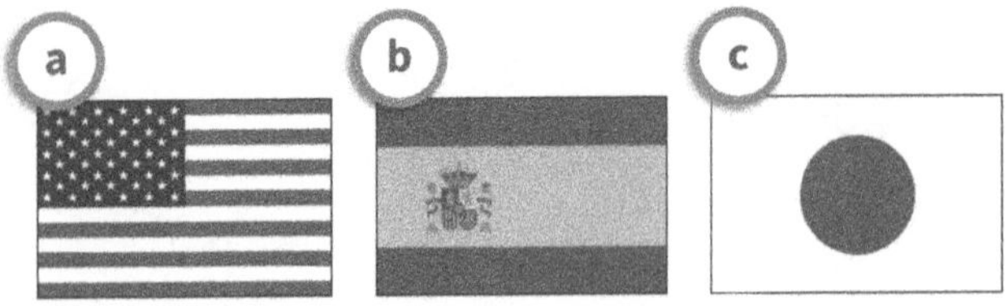

1 **Match the flags (a–c) with the countries (1–3).**

1 Spain ___ 2 Japan ___ 3 the USA ___

S.01 2 **Listen to the conversation. Which of the countries in Exercise 1 does the girl's dad sometimes go to?**

____

S.01 3 **Listen again. Put the pictures (a–f) in the order that they are mentioned.**

4 **Answer the questions.**

1 Which country would you like to visit? Why?

____

2 Would you like to travel a lot for your job? Why?

____

3 Do you think people smile a lot in your country? Give a reason for your answer.

____

Present perfect and past simple

5 **Complete the sentences with the words in the box. There are two extra words.**

at	ever	for	from	~~have~~	never	's	since

1 ___Have___ you finished the book?
2 We've been here ________ four o'clock.
3 Have you ________ been to Japan?
4 John's studied French ________ three years.
5 I've ________ seen snow before.
6 Beth ________ sent me a message.

6 **Circle the correct options.**

1 Last year I *went* / *'ve been* to London.
2 *Did you ever climb* / *Have you ever climbed* a mountain?
3 My sister *liked* / *'s liked* chocolate since she was a baby.
4 I *didn't do* / *haven't done* my homework. I'm going to start now!
5 I *phoned* / *'ve phoned* you just a minute ago!
6 We *were* / *'ve been* at the shops for three hours now!

7 **Complete the text with the past simple or present perfect form of the verb in brackets.**

TO: Aidan
FROM: Katie

Hi Aidan,

I [1] *'ve been* (be) in Rome for almost a week now. I [2] ________ (arrive) last Friday. My Italian [3] ________ (not get) much better, which isn't very surprising, really. I need more time. I [4] ________ (do) lots of sightseeing! Yesterday I [5] ________ (go) to the Vatican. The museum is incredible! I [6] ________ (eat) some very good food because the lady I'm staying with is a great cook. Last night she [7] ________ (make) cannelloni al ragù. Tomorrow, I start at the language school. I [8] ________ (not feel) so happy or excited for a long time!

Katie

WRITING

An informal email

1 ☆ **Read Jack's email to his friend Ethan. Which two of the activities in the pictures (a–c) did he do?**

a 

b 

c 

TO: Ethan@postit.co.uk

FROM: Jack@comunica.com

SUBJECT: News!

[1]<u>Hi</u> Ethan,

A [2]<u>How are things</u>? Are you enjoying life in Mexico? [3]<u>I just wanted to get in contact</u> because I haven't sent you an email for a long time. Sorry about that!

B I've been quite busy recently. I'm in the school play, and we've had lots of rehearsals after school. I've got a big part, so it hasn't been easy to learn all my lines! But I think I've finally managed to do it. I hope so, because the play's next week! Have you ever done any acting? Perhaps you can give me some advice!

C Last Saturday was my dad's 50th birthday, so he took us all out for a meal in a lovely restaurant in the country. All his brothers and sisters came, and everyone gave him a present. I gave him a Manchester United football scarf because he's a big fan. I think he liked it!

D So, that's my news. When are you coming back for Christmas?

[4]<u>Bye for now!</u>

[5]<u>Take care</u>,

Jack

2 ☆☆ **Read the email again. Match the paragraphs (A–D) with the information (1–4).**

1 Say goodbye ☐
2 Things Jack has done recently ☐
3 Things Jack did at a particular time ☐
4 Say hello and why you're writing ☐

3 ☆☆ **Look at paragraphs B and C again. What tenses does Jack use to describe his actions? Why?**

____

4 ☆☆ **Match the <u>underlined</u> expressions in the email (1–5) with the expressions (a–e).**

a Love, ☐
b I'm writing to ☐
c Hello ☐
d See you soon! ☐
e How are you? ☐

Write an email to a friend in England telling them what you've done recently.

PLAN

5 ☆☆ **Make two lists.**

1 **Things that I've done when the exact time is not important, or which are not finished** (present perfect)
I've played a lot of video games.

2 **Things that I did at a particular time** (past simple)
I played a great new video game last Tuesday.

WRITE

6 ☆☆☆ **Write your email. Remember to include four paragraphs, your ideas from Exercise 5, vocabulary from this unit and phrases from the *Useful language* box (see Student's Book, p9).**

CHECK

7 **Do you …**

- **start and end the email correctly?**
- **give the reason why you are writing?**
- **use verbs in the correct tense?**

1 TRENDSETTERS

VOCABULARY

Describing clothes and shoes

1 ☆ **Circle the correct adjectives to describe the clothes.**

1 
a *cotton* / *denim* skirt

2 
a *tight* / *baggy* jumper

3 
a *plain* / *checked* shirt

4 
flat / *high-heeled* shoes

5 
a *striped* / *flowery* T-shirt

6 
a *long-sleeved* / *spotted* dress

2 ☆☆ **Complete the conversations with the words in the box. There are two extra words.**

cotton checked denim flat flowery high-heeled long-sleeved ~~tight~~

1 A Are those shorts OK?
  B No, I need a bigger size. They're very __tight__!
2 A Do you want a plain or a checked T-shirt?
  B No, I want something really different! That ________ one is nice!
3 A What do you usually wear in the summer?
  B Cool clothes made of ________!
4 A Do you like my new black and white ________ shirt?
  B Not really! It looks like a chess board!
5 A Are you going to pack some jeans for your trip to Córdoba?
  B Are you joking? It's 40ºC there at the moment! I don't want to wear anything made of ________!
6 A How often do you wear ________ shoes?
  B Not often. Only when I go to a party or formal dinner.

3 ☆ **Circle the odd word out. Use the categories in brackets to help you. (See the *Learn to learn* tip in the Student's book, p11.)**

1 baggy — flat — tight (size)
2 checked — striped — cotton (pattern)
3 denim — flowery — cotton (material)
4 high-heeled — spotted — flat (shape)
5 long-sleeved — plain — checked (pattern)

4 ☆☆ **Write the words in the correct order.**

1 a / checked / red and green / shirt
  a red and green checked shirt
2 a / skirt / denim / plain
  ____
3 trousers / cotton / tight / white
  ____
4 jacket / denim / red / baggy / a
  ____
5 striped / brown and blue / T-shirt / a / tight / cotton
  ____
6 brown and white / shoes / leather / spotted / flat
  ____

5 ☆☆☆ **Write four sentences about clothes that you like / don't like to wear. Use the adjectives in Exercise 1.**

____
____
____
____

Explore it!

Guess the correct answer. In what decade did miniskirts become popular?
a the 1950s b the 1960s c the 1970s

Find out about popular fashion in a past decade. Then send a question in an email to a classmate or ask them in the next class.

READING

A blog post

1 ☆ **Look at the text quickly and circle the correct answers.**

1 The text is a *newspaper article / blog post.*

2 It's about *how often to wash jeans / what jeans to buy.*

2 ☆☆ **Read the blog post. Check the meaning of the words in the box in a dictionary. Then complete the sentences.**

brand	claim	harm	~~reckon~~	research	turn out

1 I *reckon* that you paid too much for that belt.

2 Don't wash that shirt in very hot water. It will definitely ________ the material!

3 I'm going to do some ________ before I buy a new phone.

4 I like these jeans, but I don't know this ________. Is it good?

5 Some people ________ that shopping online is 100% safe, but I'm not so sure.

6 I'm making a dress, but I have a feeling that it's not going to ________ well.

3 ☆☆ **Are the sentences *T* (true) or *F* (false)? Correct the false sentences.**

1 In the writer's opinion, the question of how often to wash jeans is very important.
F It's not the most important topic in the world.

2 The writer agrees with her friend about how often to wash jeans.
____

3 In the writer's opinion, an important person in the clothes industry has a strange idea.
____

4 Freezing jeans is a good way to clean them.
____

5 It's best not to wash your jeans too often.
____

6 The experts make a good recommendation.
____

4 ☆☆☆ **Do you think the information in the blog post is useful and interesting? Why?**

____
____
____

LONDON CALLING! | **BLOG** | SHOP | ABOUT ME | CONTACT ME

TO WASH OR NOT TO WASH JEANS? THAT IS THE QUESTION!

I haven't written a post recently because I've been doing exams all week! Have you missed me? Today, I want to talk about a very important subject: how often to wash denim jeans! OK, maybe it's not the most important topic in the world, but people have very different ideas about it. One of my friends even reckons that you should never wash jeans because it harms them. I don't know about that! Imagine wearing a pair of tight jeans that you haven't washed for over a year! So, anyway, I decided to do some research online about how often you should actually wash jeans. One thing I read really surprised me: the head of a company that makes a very well-known brand of jeans says that he hardly ever washes his. He just puts them in the freezer. He claims that this keeps them clean! Speaking personally, I wouldn't want to put my jeans next to a packet of frozen peas! And it turns out that the 'freezer theory' isn't correct. After you wear your jeans just once, they're covered in bacteria, skin cells and the natural oils from your body. And freezing them won't eliminate these things. According to the experts, there is one good reason for not washing your jeans very often: they get a little baggier every time you wash them. And most of us don't want to wear baggy jeans! Experts actually say there's no specific recommended frequency for washing jeans – but you should definitely wash them when they start to smell! That sounds like good advice to me!

LANGUAGE IN ACTION

Present perfect simple and present perfect continuous

1 Match the beginnings of the sentences (1–6) with the ends (a–f).

1 I've done [b]
2 Jack's been playing football [ ]
3 Have they had [ ]
4 You've been wearing [ ]
5 Bethany hasn't been going [ ]
6 Has your dad finished working [ ]

a that jumper all week!
b all my homework.
c in his study?
d for three hours!
e lunch yet?
f to the gym recently.

2 Complete the sentences with the verbs in brackets. Use the present perfect simple (PPS) or present perfect continuous (PPC).

1 We _haven't made_ (not make) lunch yet. (PPS)
2 I ____________ (do) a lot of clothes shopping recently. (PPC)
3 Ana ____________ (visit) a fashion show. (PPC)
4 ____________ (they / finish) the game? (PPS)
5 Clara ____________ (not speak) to me all day. (PPC)
6 My aunt ____________ (have) lots of different jobs. (PPS)

3 Circle the correct options.

1 I've *felt* / *(been feeling)* very tired recently.
2 John hasn't *answered* / *been answering* my last email.
3 Rachel isn't here. Has she *gone* / *been going* shopping?
4 Our neighbours have *made* / *been making* a lot of noise.
5 Why have *you bought* / *you been buying* three baggy jumpers?
6 *Did you revise* / *Have you been revising* for your exams all week?

4 Write sentences in the present perfect simple or continuous.

1 what / you do / recently?
What have you been doing recently?
2 finally / I / finish / my school project!
____
3 Nick / wear / the same clothes / all week!
____
4 you / ever/ be / to France?
____
5 I / try / to contact you / all day!
____
6 Jan / not decide / what to do
____

5 Complete the messages with the correct form of the verbs in the box.

find	go shopping	~~look for~~	not buy	try on	wait

You [1] _'ve been looking for_ a dress for the party for a long time! [2] ____________ (you) anything yet? — Maxine

No! And I [3] ____________ for hours! I [4] ____________ six different dresses, but I [5] ____________ anything yet! — Sarah

Well, I [6] ____________ for you in the café for too long! I'm going! — Maxine

6 Write a sentence about things that you have/haven't done before and a sentence about things that you have/haven't been doing recently.

I've never been to London.
I've been playing a lot of video games recently.
____
____
____
____

VOCABULARY AND LISTENING

Verbs related to clothes and shoes

1 **Circle the correct options.**

1. These trousers are very tight. They don't *fit* / *suit* me.
2. Can you please *hang* / *fit* up the trousers over there?
3. Please could you help me *undo* / *fold* the zip on my dress. I want to take it off.
4. People will still wear jeans in 100 years. They will never *wear out* / *go out of fashion*.
5. Do you think these shoes *go with* / *suit* this dress?
6. You look great with those earrings. They really *match* / *suit* you!

2 **Complete the text with the words and phrases from Exercise 1.**

HOW TO LOOK GOOD!

- Some styles [1] *go out of fashion* quickly! So, don't wear something that was popular last year!
- Your clothes must [2] ____________ you perfectly! Don't buy something that you really like if it isn't the right size!
- Buy clothes with 'easy' colours that [3] ____________ lots of other colours.
- Know what kinds of clothes [4] ____________ you! Some people look great in tight jeans – but do you?
- Don't [5] ____________ your clothes and put them in drawers. It's much better if you [6] ____________ them ____________.

3 **Write sentences that are true for you. (see the *Learn to learn* tip in the Student's Book, p14.)**

1. How quickly do you wear out your clothes?

   ____

2. Do all your clothes fit you well? Why don't they fit?

   ____

3. What colours suit you and why?

   ____

4. Do you ever wear clothes that have gone out of fashion? Why?

   ____

An interview

1.01 **4** **Listen to Caitlin talking about her job as a shop assistant. Put the things she talks about in the correct order.**

a The bad points of the job ☐
b The good points of the job ☐
c Why she wanted to work as a shop assistant ☐

1.01 **5** **Listen again and circle the correct options.**

1. Why did Caitlin decide to work as a shop assistant in a clothes shop?
   a She wants to work as a clothes designer.
   b She's very interested in clothes.
   c She likes helping people.
2. What are Caitlin's co-workers like?
   a They're nice.
   b Some are nice, some aren't.
   c She really likes her boss.
3. What happens every one or two months?
   a She buys clothes with a discount.
   b She helps with window displays.
   c New clothes arrive at the shop.
4. How much discount does Caitlin get?
   a 15%
   b 50%
   c It depends on the clothes.
5. What are two negative aspects of the job?
   a Some of the jobs are a bit boring and the pay isn't very good.
   b Some of the customers can be rude and you're standing up all the time.
   c Some customers aren't polite and not all the jobs are interesting.

LANGUAGE IN ACTION

Modifiers

1 Read the phrases and circle the options that have the same meaning.

1 absolutely wrong
 a totally wrong b a little wrong
2 fairly nice
 a extremely nice b quite nice
3 a lot more difficult
 a a bit more difficult b far more difficult
4 a bit bigger
 a a little bigger b far bigger
5 extremely tired
 a quite tired b really tired
6 pretty far
 a rather far b extremely far

2 Look at the information from a price comparison website. Are the sentences *T* (true) or *F* (false)?

1 Exclu jeans are extremely expensive. ___T___
2 Wright Brothers jeans are rather cheap. ______
3 Exclu jeans are far more expensive than Basic Co jeans. ______
4 Basic Co jeans aren't really cheap. ______
5 Wright Brothers jeans are a bit cheaper than Exclu jeans. ______
6 Basic Co jeans are quite expensive. ______

3 Circle the correct options.

1 These trousers aren't 'quite' baggy. They're *rather* / *extremely* baggy!
2 Your watch was a bit more expensive than mine, but it's *a little* / *far* better! It's fantastic!
3 I'm *quite* / *really* hungry but I'm not very hungry.
4 The weather was a *bit* / *far* hotter than we imagined. It was a big surprise.
5 Mike's *quite* / *really* generous. I think he's the most generous person I know.
6 I'm *fairly* / *totally* sure that the shop's closed today, but perhaps I'm wrong.

4 Complete the conversation with the missing words. Circle the correct options.

A How was your holiday in San Sebastian?
B Only [1] ______ good, I'm afraid.
A So, not [2] ______ fantastic?
B No. The weather was [3] ______ terrible. It rained all the time!
A Oh dear! What about the food? I've heard it's fantastic over there – [4] ______ better than the food in the UK!
B Yes, it was [5] ______ delicious! I think it was [6] ______ more expensive than the UK, but my dad said the prices weren't too bad.

	a	b	c
1	totally	fairly	far
2	a lot	quite	absolutely
3	really	a bit	rather
4	totally	far	a little
5	absolutely	pretty	a lot
6	far	quite	a bit

5 Complete the sentences so they are true for you. Use the modifiers from this page.

1 Living in my home town is ______.
2 My family is ______.
3 For me, buying clothes is ______.
4 When I compare English and maths, I think English is ______.
5 In my opinion, football is ______.
6 When I compare drinking water or cola, I think ______.

WRITING

Blog post comments

FIVE WAYS TO SPEND LESS MONEY ON CLOTHES

- Go to second-hand clothes shops!
- Buy your clothes online!
- Swap clothes with friends!
- Only buy clothes in the sales!
- Buy clothes with neutral colours (black, grey or white). They'll go well with all your other clothes!

Great post! Thanks for sharing! TBH, I've always thought that buying clothes online was a bit dangerous. I mean, what happens if you get something and it doesn't fit you? That's a problem! But since reading your post, I've looked at some online clothes sites, and they really help you to find your right size. What's more, some of the clothes are extremely cheap, especially if you buy from China or Hong Kong! I've just bought a flowery dress online and it fits me perfectly! It's absolutely amazing! Sonya

Your post really got me thinking about how to save money on clothes! I've been spending too much recently, so it's become a BIG problem! IMO going to second-hand shops is a really good idea. I had no idea that they had such great stuff! I thought they only had clothes which were out of fashion! I've already bought a great denim shirt and a cool spotted T-shirt. And I've decided to get all my clothes from second-hand shops in the future! They're far cheaper! Aidan

1 ★☆☆ **Read the blog post and the comments and answer the questions.**

1 What is the blog post about?

____

2 Which ideas from the post have Sonya and Aidan used?

____

2 ★☆☆ **Read the comments again and answer the questions.**

1 What do TBH and IMO mean? ______________

2 Why does Sonya use an exclamation mark in: *It's absolutely amazing!* ?

3 Why does Aidan use capital letters in: *It's become a BIG problem!* ?

3 ★☆☆ **Complete the *Useful language* phrases. Look at the underlined phrases in the blog for help.**

1 You have really __got__ me thinking about how much I spend.

2 I've been thinking and I've __________ to go shopping far less often.

3 Great __________! Thanks for __________!

4 I had __________ that buying online was so easy!

5 __________ reading your post, I've really started to think about how I shop.

Write your own blog post comment.

PLAN

4 ★☆☆ **Choose one of the five ideas in Exercise 1 and make notes about these things.**

Did it go well? Why / Why not? ______________

____

Which other ideas would you like to try in the future?

____

WRITE

5 ★★★ **Write your comment. Remember to include the present perfect simple and continuous, modifiers, vocabulary from this unit, phrases from the *Useful language* box (see Student's Book, p17) and the features from Exercise 2.**

CHECK

6 **Do you …**

- explain why an idea might or might not work well?
- explain what you would like to try in the future?

1 REVIEW

VOCABULARY

1 Complete the crossword. Use the clues.

ACROSS →

2 ________ T-shirt
3 ________ jumper
4 ________ scarf
6 ________ trousers
9 ________-________ dress
11 ________ shirt
12 ________ top

2

3

4

6
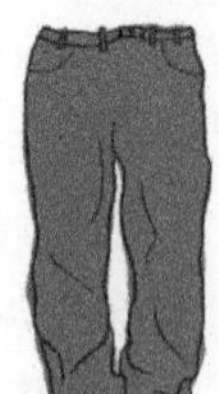

9

11

12

DOWN ↓

1 ________ shirt
5 ________-________ shoes
7 ________ skirt
8 ________ shoes
10 ________ jeans

1

5

7

8

10
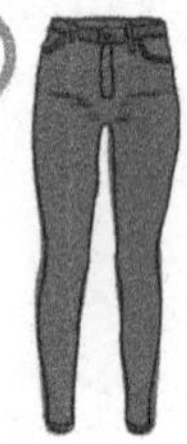

2 Complete the sentences with the words in the box.

do up fit fold go out of fashion go with hang up match suit undo wear out

1 I don't think these shoes will ____________ soon. Trainers are always popular.
2 You need to ____________ the zip on your coat. It's very cold!
3 These shorts don't ____________ me now, but they weren't too small last year!
4 Do you think these earrings ____________ the colour of my eyes?
5 I never wear brown. It doesn't ____________ me.
6 I only ____________ shirts when I pack a bag. I always ____________ them ____________ at home.
7 That shirt doesn't ____________ those trousers. They look terrible together!
8 You can ____________ the zip on the tent. It isn't raining any more.
9 Those are nice shoes, so please don't play football in them. You'll ____________ them ____________ very quickly!

LANGUAGE IN ACTION

3 Complete the sentences with the present perfect simple or continuous form of the verbs in brackets.

1 I ______ (not see) that film. Is it good?

2 Chloe ______ (try) to book tickets all afternoon!

3 Oh, no! I ______ (lose) my earring!

4 Dan ______ (never / play) chess.

5 I ______ (finish)! I'm sorry you ______ (wait) so long.

6 ______ (we / buy) everything we need?

4 Read the conversations and circle the correct options.

1 A How was the party?
  B It was *really* / *pretty* good, but not amazing.

2 A Did you enjoy the film?
  B Yes, it was *fairly* / *absolutely* brilliant!

3 A How are you feeling?
  B Only *a little* / *a lot* better.

4 A Did you do well in your exams?
  B My results were *extremely* / *quite* good, but they weren't fantastic.

5 A This school project is hard!
  B Yes, it is! It's *fairly* / *far* harder than Ms Taylor said!

6 A I'm the best player in the team!
  B I'm sorry, but you're *rather* / *totally* wrong about that!

CUMULATIVE LANGUAGE

5 Complete the email with the missing words. Circle the correct options.

TO: Amy FROM: Zoe

Hi Amy,

How are you? I'm sorry that I [1] ______ for a while. I've got lots of news! I [2] ______ a course in fashion design and it [3] ______ really well! I [4] ______ on a dress with a flowery design all week. I [5] ______ it because it's [6] ______ hard work. But I love it! I [7] ______ that I want to work as a fashion designer in the future. I think it would be a [8] ______ brilliant job – and [9] ______ more interesting than working in an office! How about you? [10] ______ life in Chile? Your Spanish must be [11] ______ fantastic now because it was [12] ______ good before!

Anyway, speak soon!

Zoe

	a	b	c
1	haven't written	haven't been writing	don't write
2	've been starting	start	've started
3	's gone	goes	's been going
4	work	've been working	've worked
5	haven't finished	don't finish	haven't been finishing
6	far	a little	really
7	decide	've decided	've been deciding
8	fairly	far	totally
9	far	quite	a bit
10	Do you enjoy	Have you been enjoying	Have you enjoyed
11	rather	a lot	absolutely
12	pretty	well	a lot

2 CHANGES

VOCABULARY

Phrasal verbs: changes

1 Circle the correct options.

1 Max has settled (down) / *up* well at his new school.
2 I'm really *looking* / *seeing* forward to next weekend.
3 I'm going to sign *up* / *down* for yoga classes.
4 Let's *try* / *do* out the new skate park.
5 I'm *having* / *going* through a hard time at the moment.
6 Are you going to turn *up* / *down* Jack's invitation?

2 Complete the sentences with the phrasal verbs in the box.

do without	end up	go back
move out	~~sign up~~	turn out

1 Did you sign up for the school trip to Paris?
2 The party didn't ________ very well in the end. Not many people came.
3 My sister wants to ________ and be more independent.
4 If you don't work hard at school, you probably won't ________ with a good job.
5 I don't think I could ________ chocolate! I love it!
6 I probably won't ________ to my home town when I finish university.

3 Complete the personality questionnaire with the correct form of the verbs in the box and the correct prepositions.

do go look forward ~~move~~ move sign try turn

Are you a positive person?

1 Would you like to move out of your family's home before you're 25?
2 In your life, do things usually ________ well?
3 When you are ________ a hard time, do you look for solutions?
4 Do you ________ for lots of optional activities at school?
5 Do you like to ________ new ways of doing things?
6 When you get up, do you always ________ everything you will do in the day?
7 Would you like to ________ a new country?
8 Could you ________ the Internet for a week?

4 Answer *Yes* or *No* to the questions in Exercise 3. How positive are you?

7–8 *yes* answers: very positive!
5–6 *yes* answers: quite positive!
Less than 5 *yes* answers: not very positive!

5 Write four sentences with phrasal verbs about what kind of person you are. (See the *Learn to learn* tip in the Student's Book, p23.)

____
____
____
____

Explore it!

Guess the correct answer. What is the minimum age when you can start working in the UK without your parents' permission?

Find out about when you can legally do something for the first time in your country or in the UK. Then email a question to a classmate or ask them in the next class.

READING

A blog post

1 ☆ **Look at the blog post quickly. Why is Chloe's life new? Tick (✓) the correct answer.**

a She's just got married. ☐
b She's at university now. ☐
c She's just finished university. ☐

2 ☆☆ **Read the blog post and check the meaning of the words in the box in a dictionary. Then complete the sentences.**

~~disappointed~~ keen lecture law plenty of surrounded

1 I did badly in my exams. I'm really *disappointed* !
2 I'm very ______ to move out, but I haven't got the money now!
3 The campsite was ______ by trees, so it was very beautiful.
4 My cousin's studying ______. He says it's lots of work.
5 I know ______ people, but do I have any real friends?
6 I've just been to a really interesting ______.

3 ☆☆ **Read the first paragraph of the blog post and answer the questions. Write 'no information' if there is no answer in the text.**

1 Which university is Chloe going to?
______
2 What does Chloe mean when she says that you 'have to start from zero'?
______
3 Why are things turning out well?
______

4 ☆☆ **Read the second paragraph of the blog post and complete the table.**

	Studying at school	Studying at university
1	*classes in small groups*	
2		
3		

5 ☆☆☆ **Do you think it's a good idea to study away from home? Write three or four sentences.**

______
______
______
______

CHLOE'S CORNER | **BLOG** | **ABOUT** | **FAQS**

A NEW LIFE!

Have you ever had a really special time in your life? Well, I'm having one now because I've just started university! I was really looking forward to it and, so far, I haven't been disappointed! My principal worry before coming was: would it be easy to make new friends? It's a good question because, when you go to uni, you have to start from zero. The old friends you used to see at home aren't there anymore, so you need to create a completely new social life. Well, I'm glad to say that things are turning out really well. I'm living in a hall of residence, which is a special building just for students. It's the ideal place to be in your first year because you're surrounded by new faces! And everyone's keen to make new friends.

Studying at university feels very different from how things used to be at school. Although there were a lot of students at school, there are over 100 students at my lectures. At school, we would have the chance to ask questions and to discuss things with our teachers. Now you just sit down and take notes! Another big difference is that I only have 12 hours of lectures per week (I'm studying law). The rest of the time I spend studying alone. That can be quite difficult because you need a lot of discipline! And there are plenty of other, more interesting things to do!

I've settled down really well to university life. There's just one 'small' problem: I need to study more!

LANGUAGE IN ACTION

used to, *would* and past simple

1 ★★ **Complete the sentences with the correct form of *used to* and the verbs in brackets.**

1 I <u>used to hate</u> (hate) going to the dentist.
2 My dad ______________ (have) more hair.
3 I ______________ (not like) carrots.
4 My mum ______________ (not go) to the gym.
5 ______________ (you / play) the violin?
6 ______________ (Matt / be) your best friend?

2 ★★ **Rewrite the sentences with *used to* when it is possible.**

1 I went to bed at ten o'clock last night.
<u>not possible</u>
2 In the past, did your granddad ride a bike to work?
____
3 People went to the cinema more often before the Internet.
____
4 Clothes didn't wear out so quickly before.
____
5 Oh, no! Did you leave the keys at home?
____
6 Was there a castle in this town before?
____

3 ★★★ **Write four sentences about what people *used to* / *didn't use to* do. Use the photos for ideas.**

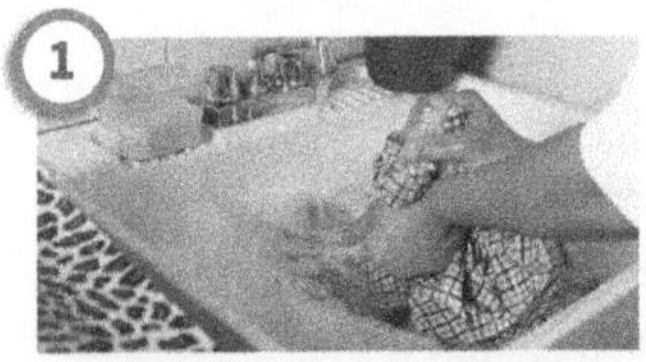

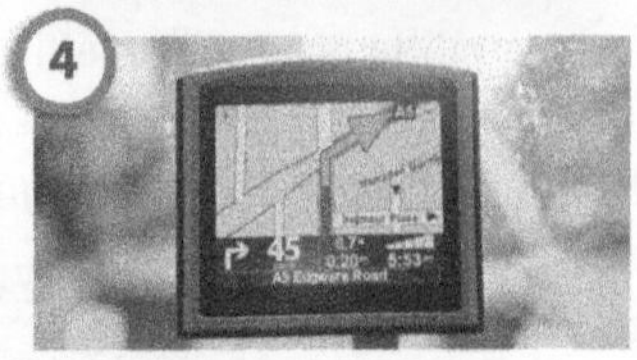

____
____
____
____

4 ★ **Circle the correct options.**

Things were different when I was young!

Children [1](would) / *wouldn't* listen to their parents and teachers. Now they don't listen!

People [2]*would* / *wouldn't* run everywhere. They had more time.

We [3]*would* / *wouldn't* play on the street. It wasn't dangerous then.

People [4]*would* / *wouldn't* think about money all the time. They had better values.

Families [5]*would* / *wouldn't* go abroad on holiday. And some families didn't go anywhere!

We [6]*would* / *wouldn't* listen to the radio more because not everyone had a TV.

5 ★★ **Rewrite the <u>underlined</u> part of the sentences with *would*. If it isn't possible, rewrite the sentences with *used to*.**

1 <u>We lived</u> in the country before.
<u>We used to live in the country before.</u>
2 <u>I often arrived</u> late for school when I was younger.
____
3 <u>Did you wear</u> glasses before?
____
4 <u>My grandma always went</u> for a walk after breakfast.
____
5 <u>My dad often swam</u> in the sea when he lived in Cádiz.
____
6 <u>My mum was</u> a nurse before.
____

6 ★★ **Circle the correct option OR options.**

A [1]*Did you have* / *Did you use to have* tennis lessons?
B Yes, I did.
A So, why [2]*did* / *would* you stop?
B My teacher [3]*would* / *used to* criticise me all the time. So, one day I [4]*decided* / *used to decide*, 'No more tennis lessons!'
A Really? I [5]*didn't* / *didn't use to* know anything about that! Who [6]*did you* / *did you use to* have lessons with?
B My dad!

VOCABULARY AND LISTENING

Parts of objects

1 ☆ **Find nine more parts of objects in the word search.**

b	o	l	s	l	e	n	s
h	b	u	t	t	o	n	o
a	t	h	r	o	o	s	p
n	r	c	a	b	l	e	l
d	i	m	p	l	a	y	u
l	l	c	o	v	e	r	g
e	i	h	k	e	y	o	u
t	d	i	s	p	l	a	y

2 ☆☆ **Complete the sentences with words from Exercise 1.**

1 Oh no! A *strap* on my backpack has broken.
2 There's a problem with the ______ on my phone. It's very dark.
3 These photos have turned out badly because the ______ on my camera was dirty.
4 Let's carry this bag together. You take one ______ and I'll take the other.
5 Where's the ______ for the saucepan?
6 Is this the ______ for your mobile phone's cable?
7 This ______ on my laptop is for changing the audio volume.
8 The ______ of this book looks really great, but the book wasn't very interesting!
9 You need to attach this ______ to the printer.

3 ☆☆☆ **Write a description of a 'mystery object'. Use at least four of the words from Exercise 1. Send your description in an email to a classmate or ask them to guess the object in the next class.**

It's got a display and it's got one or two buttons, but it hasn't got a plug. It hasn't got a handle, but it's got a strap. What is it?

______

______

______

A conversation

2.01 **4** ☆ **Listen to a conversation about the past between Katie and her gran. Tick (✓) the things they mention.**

1 a plug ✓

2 a calculator ☐

3 a video cassette ☐

4 a TV ☐

5 a camera ☐

6 a PowerPoint presentation ☐

5 ☆ **Underline the key words in the sentences. (See the *Learn to learn* tip in the Student's Book, p26.)**

1 Katie is going to work on a history project. *F*
2 Her gran thinks that young people spend too much time using 'technological things'. ___
3 Katie's gran didn't use a calculator at school. ___
4 There weren't many programmes on TV before. ___
5 Katie thinks that life before sounds fun. ___
6 When her gran was at school, each student had a small blackboard to write on. ___

2.01 **6** ☆☆ **Listen again. Are the sentences in Exercise 5 *T* (true) or *F* (false)?**

7 ☆☆☆ **What three modern inventions couldn't you do without?**

______

______

LANGUAGE IN ACTION

Past perfect with *never, already, by (then), by the time*

1 ☆ **Read the sentences and underline the action that happened first.**

1 I had already had lunch when my sister arrived.
2 My sister had already got married by the time she was 20.
3 Dan wasn't happy because I had turned down his invitation.
4 By the time the match finished, we had scored five goals!
5 We had walked a very long way by the time we found the river.

2 ☆☆ **Match the beginnings of the sentences (1–5) with the ends (a–e).**

1 I had never seen snow [*c*]
2 We had only been at the hotel a few minutes when [ ]
3 Had you ever run more than 5 km [ ]
4 By the time my granddad settled in England, [ ]
5 We had already been to six different shops [ ]

a by the time Clara decided to buy something.
b before today?
c before I went to Sierra Nevada.
d he'd lived in six different countries.
e the storm started.

3 ☆☆ **Put the words in the correct order to make sentences.**

1 car / seen / had / the / already
I *had already seen the car.*
2 had / then / back / by / come
Jack ______
3 rang / woken up / you / I / when / already / ?
Had ______
4 abroad / never / year / had / last / been / I
Before ______
5 then / a snake / ever / you / before / seen / ?
Had ______

4 ☆☆ **Complete the sentences with the past simple or the past perfect.**

1 Pablo *had never had* (never / have) guitar lessons before he *gave* (give) his first concert.
2 ______ (Sean / ever make) lasagne before today?
3 School ______ (already / start) when I ______ (arrive).
4 By the time Sara ______ (leave) England, she ______ (learn) to speak English very well.
5 I ______ (never / feel) real terror until I ______ (see) that film!
6 ______ (everyone / already / go) to bed by the time the fire ______ (start)?

5 ☆☆☆ **Complete the text with the past simple or the past perfect.**

Emma [1] *moved* (move) to a new school last year. By the time she [2] ______ (be) there a couple of weeks, she [3] ______ (already / settle) down very well. And now things are going even better! Last week she [4] ______ (become) the captain of the school football team.

She [5] ______ (be) very happy about this because she [6] ______ (always / want) to be the team captain. And yesterday she [7] ______ (receive) her exam results. More good news! She [8] ______ (never / get) all top marks before!

6 ☆☆☆ **Complete the sentences with your own ideas. Use the past perfect.**

1 Before this year, I ______
2 We didn't win the match because we ______
3 I signed up for karate lessons because ______
4 By the time Ella finished university, ______
5 Max was going through a hard time because ______

WRITING

An opinion essay

1 ☆ **Look at the essay quickly. Does the writer think that life used to be better in the past?**

____

2 ☆☆ **Read the essay and answer the questions. Tick (✓) and circle the correct answers.**

1 In which TWO paragraphs does the writer give ideas to support their opinion?

A ☐ B ☐ C ☐ D ☐

2 In paragraph A, the writer *asks a question / gives their opinion*.

3 In paragraph D, the writer *repeats their opinion / asks the reader a question.*

3 ☆☆ **Complete the essay with the *Useful language* phrases in the box.**

~~firstly~~ in addition in conclusion secondly therefore this means that

4 ☆☆ **What different words or expressions does the writer use to avoid repeating items 1–4 below?**

1 in the past (paragraph B) ______________

2 better (paragraph B) ______________

3 situation (paragraph B) ______________

4 look at (paragraph D) ______________

5 ☆☆ **Complete the sentence.**

In paragraphs B and C, to describe life in the past, the writer uses the past simple, ______________ and ______________.

Did life use to be better?

A Older people often say that, in the past, life used to be better. However, in my opinion, this is simply not true.

B [1] ___Firstly___, let's look at the situation of women. In the old days, many men (and some women) used to think that a woman's role in life was to be a mother and to do the housework and the cooking. Fortunately, attitudes have changed a lot since then! [2] ______________ women today are in a much more favourable position.

C [3] ______________, the number of very poor people around the world has decreased significantly in the last 20 or 30 years. [4] ______________, many children in poor countries would die when they were still very young. This happens far less often now. [5] ______________ we can talk about huge change in two very important areas.

D [6] ______________, the world today is a much better place. If we examine the facts, no one would want to go back to a 'golden past'. This past only exists in some people's imagination. It never existed in reality.

Write an opinion essay.

PLAN

6 ☆☆ **Look at the statement. In your notebook, write down three reasons why you agree or disagree with it.**

It's more important to speak English today than in the past.

____

____

____

WRITE

7 ☆☆☆ **Write your opinion essay. Remember to include four paragraphs, and examples of *used to*, *would*, the past simple, past perfect and the *Useful language* phrases from Exercise 3.**

CHECK

8 **Do you ...**

- give your opinion?
- give reasons for your opinion?
- summarise your opinion?

2 REVIEW

LANGUAGE IN ACTION

1 Rewrite the second sentence so that it has a similar meaning to the first. Use the phrasal verbs in the box.

do without	go back	go through	look forward to	move to	settle down	try out	turn down

1 Let's return to the bus station.
Let's ______________ the bus station.

2 I'm very excited about the concert on Saturday.
I'm ______________ the concert on Saturday.

3 I have to have a shower.
I can't ______________ every morning.

4 I'm sorry, but I can't accept your invitation.
I'm sorry, but I have to ______________.

5 Mike's adapting well to life in Milan.
Mike's ______________ in Milan.

6 Bethany isn't enjoying life at all at the moment.
Bethany is ______________ a hard time at the moment.

7 Jack used to live in London, but he went to live in Manchester.
Jack ______________ Manchester.

8 Let's see what this new video game is like!
Let's ______________ video game!

2 Complete the crossword. Use the picture clues.

Across →

3

4
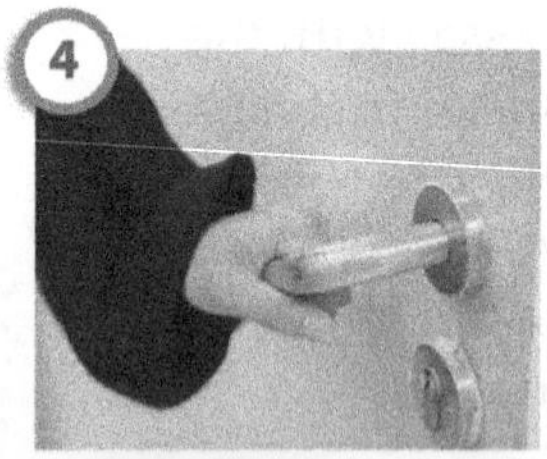

6
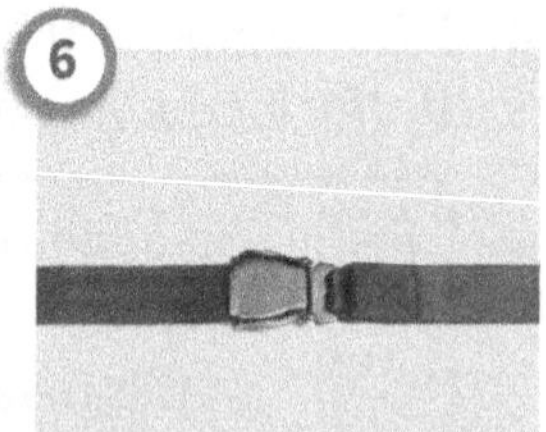

8

9

Down ↓

1

2

3
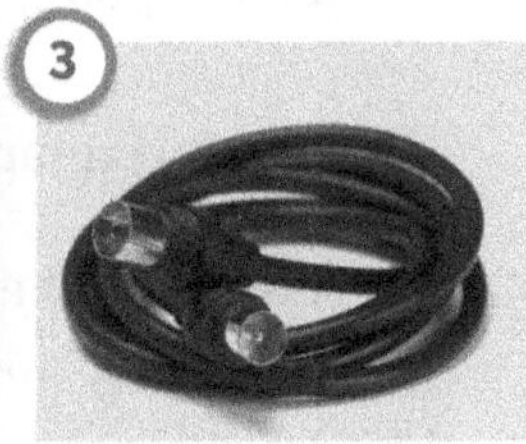

5

7
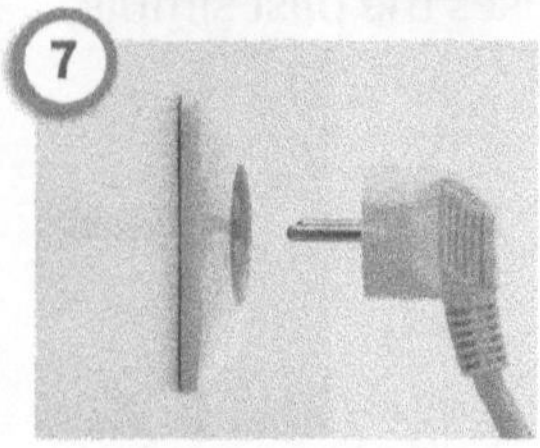

LANGUAGE IN ACTION

3 Complete the text with *used to*, *would* or the past simple of the words in brackets.

When my mum was ten, she [1] ______ (get) a cat for her birthday. She loved the cat and it [2] ______ (follow) her everywhere. The cat [3] ______ (explore) other people's gardens and he [4] ______ (fight) with other cats from time to time. Then one day, the cat [5] ______ (not come) home. Mum [6] ______ (be) so sad – she [7] ______ (put up) posters to try and find him. Finally, he came home five days later. Mum was very happy!

4 Circle the sentence (A or B) that has a similar meaning to the first.

1 The train had already left when we got to the station.
   - A When we got to the station, the train left.
   - B We arrived at the station late, so we missed the train.

2 Before we went to Turkey last year, I'd never been there.
   - A Last year was the first time I was in Turkey.
   - B I didn't visit Turkey last year.

3 By the time I learned to drive, I'd spent lots of money on driving lessons.
   - A I spent a lot of money before I could drive.
   - B I learned to drive before I spent a lot of money.

4 Amy hadn't finished her homework when Aidan came.
   - A Aidan arrived and Amy finished her homework.
   - B When Aidan came, Amy was still doing her homework.

5 Ryan had never seen a lion before he went to the zoo last week.
   - A Ryan didn't see a lion at the zoo.
   - B Before his trip to the zoo last week, Ryan hadn't seen a lion.

6 We had taken lots of photos by the time our holiday was over.
   - A We took a lot of photos on holiday.
   - B When our holiday finished, we took lots of photos.

CUMULATIVE LANGUAGE

5 Complete the text with the missing words. Circle the correct options.

Joe said, 'I [1] ______ to this new school a month ago, but I [2] ______ down to life here very well.' '[3] ______ through a hard time?' I asked him. 'Yes, I [4] ______,' he said. 'It's been [5] ______ difficult. At my old school, I [6] ______ lots of friends. And I [7] ______ them very often after school. Before I came here, I [8] ______ that it would be so hard to make new friends. It's been [9] ______ harder than I thought.' '[10] ______ up for any school clubs?' I asked. 'Yes, I [11] ______ to two or three different ones,' Joe replied. 'You know, I [12] ______ quite popular at my old school,' he continued. 'Nothing like this [13] ______ to me before.'

	a	b	c
1	moved	had moved	used to move
2	didn't settle	haven't settled	hadn't settled
3	Did you go	Had you gone	Have you been going
4	did	have	been
5	far	absolutely	really
6	would have	used to have	have had
7	had seen	have been seeing	would see
8	hadn't expected	haven't expected	wouldn't expect
9	pretty	totally	far
10	Did you sign	Have you signed	Had you signed
11	've been going	had gone	would go
12	used to be	would be	've been
13	had happened	has happened	has been happening

3 FOOD FOR THOUGHT

VOCABULARY

Cooking verbs

1 ☆ Find 11 more verbs for cooking in the word search.

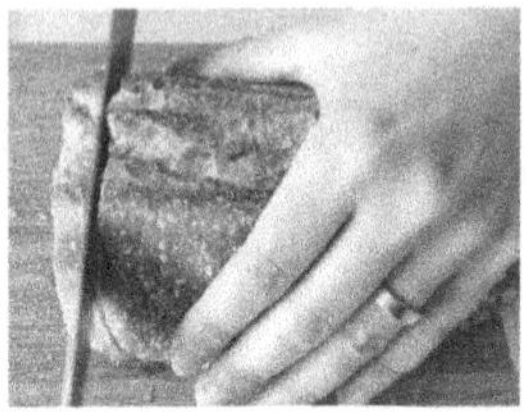

c	h	o	p	o	p	e	e	l
r	o	v	g	r	i	l	l	d
i	s	e	a	s	o	n	s	i
s	p	r	e	a	d	o	l	h
h	o	c	r	a	m	f	i	e
a	r	o	a	s	t	f	c	a
r	e	o	v	e	r	r	e	t
b	a	k	e	m	y	y	o	t
o	m	u	g	r	a	t	e	e

2 ☆ Circle the verb that goes with the food.

1 *grate* / *peel* cheese
2 *bake* / *heat* milk
3 *peel* / *season* an apple
4 *grate* / *roast* a chicken
5 *spread* / *roast* butter
6 *chop* / *slice* bread
7 *grate* / *fry* eggs
8 *peel* / *overcook* fish

3 ☆☆ Complete the sentences with the words in the box.

bake chop grill ~~overcook~~ season spread

1 Please don't *overcook* the meat. One or two minutes is enough.
2 ________ the onions into small pieces.
3 Do you often ________ bread in the oven?
4 When you barbecue, you ________ meat over a fire.
5 ________ the dish with salt and pepper.
6 Have you got a knife to ________ the jam?

4 ☆☆ Complete the recipe with the words in the box.

fry grate heat overcook season ~~slice~~ spread

A fantastic snack

[1] *Slice* some bread and toast it. Take some paté and [2] ________ it on the bread. [3] ________ some cheese and put it on the paté. In a pan, [4] ________ some oil. Then, put an egg in the pan and [5] ________ it for only one or two minutes. Don't [6] ________ it! Put the egg on the bread. [7] ________ with black pepper. It's ready to eat!

5 ☆☆☆ Write how to make something simple (e.g. an omelette, a milkshake, your favourite sandwich).

____

____

____

____

6 ☆☆ Write the adjective form of the verbs in Exercise 2 in the table. (See the *Learn to learn* tip in the Student's Book, p35.)

-ed ending	other
grated,	

Explore it!

Guess the correct answer.
What is the main ingredient of this dish called Bombay Duck?
a duck b horse meat c fish

Find the answers to the questions:
1 What is bubble and squeak?
2 When do people in England have it?

READING

An online forum

1 ☆ Match the photos (1–4) with the four comments on the online forum (A–D).

2 ☆☆ Read the text and check the meaning of the words in the box in a dictionary. Then complete the sentences.

~~costume~~ freezing highlight hiking melt sensible

1 What *costume* are you going to wear to the fancy-dress party?
2 Riding your bike at night without lights is not ________ at all.
3 Eat your ice cream quickly or it'll ________!
4 My friend Mia goes ________ even in the middle of winter!
5 It's ________ outside, so put on a warm coat.
6 The ________ of the meal was when they brought out my birthday cake.

3 ☆☆ Complete the article with the missing sentence parts (a–f).

a The food was OK
b and they read some poems
c because it's so incredibly beautiful
d My sister doesn't eat meat
e ~~The highlight of the trip was when we went to an undersea restaurant~~
f in the summer

4 ☆☆☆ Which of the four places would you most like to eat at? Why? Write three or four sentences.

____
____
____
____
____
____
____

1

2

3

4

ASK IT! HOME ANSWER NOTIFICATIONS SEARCH

Where's the most memorable place you've ever eaten?

A My dad won £100,000 on the lottery and he decided to do something very sensible with it: he took all of us on holiday to the Maldive Islands! (They're about 400 miles south-west of India.) [1] *e* . Beautiful tropical fish swam past as we ate! It was an experience that I'll never forget! [2] ________, but nothing special.

Sam, London

B In the north of Finland, there's a fantastic snow hotel with a restaurant made of ice! It's only open in the winter. Perhaps it melts [3] ________! You need to wear warm clothes or you're going to be freezing because you sit on ice chairs all the time! We had grilled salmon (very good!), but the roast meat for the main course was a bit overcooked. Oh well, nowhere's perfect!

Oona, Helsinki

C When we were on holiday in Ireland, we went for a medieval dinner at Bunratty Castle. It was a lot of fun! They had actors in traditional costumes, [4] ________. There was also Irish music. The food was good, but we didn't eat with our hands like in Medieval times! They did vegetarian food, too. [5] ________ and she loved the baked carrots with grated cheese.

Charlotte, Bristol

D The most memorable place I've eaten was Pulpit Rock in Norway. The meal wasn't exactly spectacular – a sandwich, an energy bar and an apple! But the view *was* spectacular! You could see for miles! And the food didn't taste bad after hiking for a couple of hours! It's not easy to get to Pulpit Rock from Ireland. But I might go back a second time [6] ________!

Conor, Dublin

LANGUAGE IN ACTION

Future tenses

1 ★ **Match the verbs in sentences 1–6 with the uses (a–c).**

1 We're meeting at six o'clock. [c]
2 The bus leaves at 10 am. [ ]
3 I'm going to study more this year. [ ]
4 Are you and Jack playing tennis tonight? [ ]
5 The restaurant opens at 7 pm. [ ]
6 Zoe's going to try to make lasagna. [ ]

a To talk about future plans and intentions
b To talk about scheduled or timetabled events
c To talk about fixed arrangements in the future

2 ★★ **Circle the correct options.**

1 What *do you do* / *(are you doing)* tonight?
2 The match *starts* / *is starting* in five minutes!
3 My sister *learns* / *is going to learn* to drive next year.
4 We *meet* / *'re meeting* in the park at six o'clock.
5 I *make* / *'m going to make* dinner in a few minutes.
6 Joel *has* / *is going to have* a piano lesson in a few minutes.
7 *I'm getting* / *'m going to get* my green belt in judo this year. It's my big goal for the year.
8 We *go* / *'re going* skateboarding this weekend.

3 ★★★ **Write about two fixed future arrangements that you have / haven't made and two future intentions that you have / don't have.**

____

____

____

____

4 ★ **Match the underlined verbs in sentences 1–3 with the uses (a–c).**

1 Those biscuits smell amazing. And I'm sure <u>they're going to taste</u> delicious! [ ]
2 More people <u>will become</u> vegetarians in the future. [ ]
3 I <u>might want</u> some more pizza. Let me finish this first! [ ]

a a future prediction that we don't feel sure about
b a future prediction based on evidence in the present
c a future prediction that we feel sure about

5 ★★ **Complete the predictions with *be going to*, *will* or *may*/*might* and the verbs in the box.**

come	have	love	~~miss~~	not cost	not finish

1 Oh, no! It's 5.59! We *'re going to miss* the six o'clock train!
2 John ____________ to the party. Let's wait and see!
3 I'm sure Deborah ____________ the present you chose for her. You have great taste.
4 This meal ____________ a lot! Prices are cheap!
5 Some experts say that one day everyone in the world ____________ enough food to eat.
6 I ____________ this book tonight, but I'm going to try.

6 ★★★ **Complete the conversation with the correct form of the verbs in brackets. Use the present simple, present continuous, *be going to*, *will* or *may*/*might*.**

A I [1] *'m never going to cook* (never / cook) a big meal again!
B Why? It wasn't so bad. And I'm sure your cooking [2] ____________ (get) better in the future.
A Hmm … I suppose I [3] ____________ (make) some progress.
B Don't be so negative! Anyway, what [4] ____________ (you / do) after lunch?
A I [5] ____________ (go) to the cinema with Will. The film [6] ____________ (start) at 5 pm.

7 ★★★ **Complete the sentences with your own ideas.**

1 In ten years' time, I might ______________________________
______________________________.
2 In 100 years, everyone will ______________________________
______________________________.
3 I might ______________________________
______________________________.

VOCABULARY AND LISTENING

Quantities

1 Circle the correct expression of quantity to describe each photo.

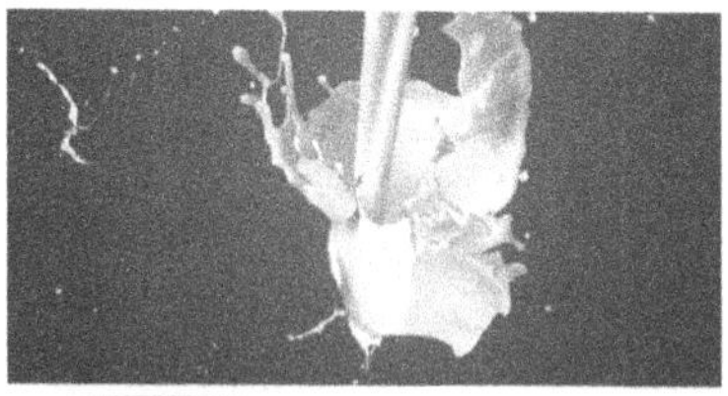

1 *a splash* / *cup* of milk

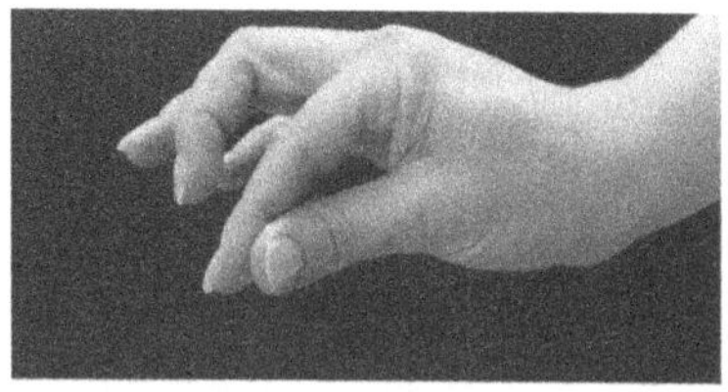

2 a *packet* / *pinch* of salt

3 a *spoonful* / *packet* of sugar

4 a *slice* / *piece* of bread

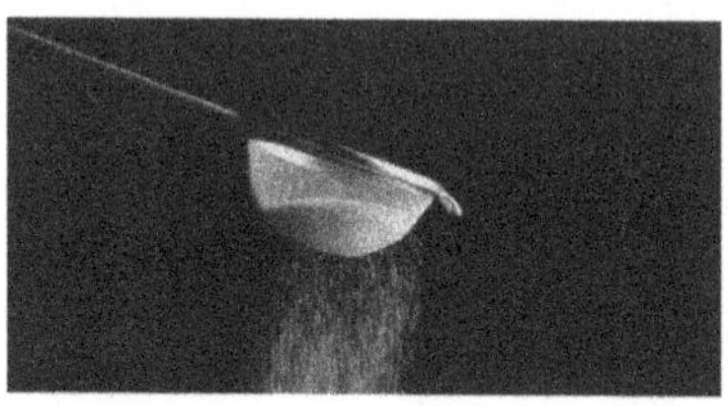

5 a *sprinkle* / *handful* of sugar

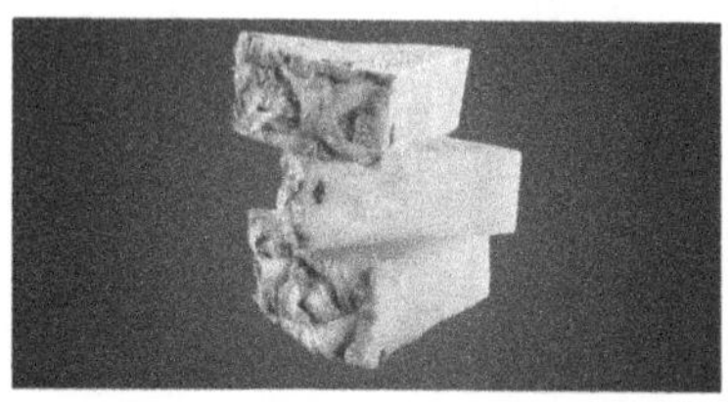

6 *slices* / *chunks* of pineapple

2 Complete the table with the quantities in the box. (see the *Learn to learn* tip in the Student's Book, p38.)

a cup of   a handful of   a packet of   a piece of
a pinch of   a slice of   a splash of   a spoonful of
a sprinkle of   ~~chunks of~~

sugar	milk	cheese
		chunks of

3 Write about three things you like to eat or drink. Use the expressions of quantity in Exercise 2.

I love two slices of toast and jam for breakfast.

____

____

____

An interview

3.01 **4 Listen to a man talking about his job. Are the sentences *T* (true) or *F* (false)?**

1 James has his own food shop. ___
2 James works a lot. ___
3 His job has several good points. ___
4 He never has time to eat the food that he cooks. ___

3.01 **5 Listen again and complete the sentences with ONE word from the interview.**

1 James works in the city of London.
2 In the restaurant there can be ________ people eating at the same time.
3 The food needs to arrive at customers' tables quickly and the dishes need to be ________ quality.
4 James doesn't ________ down very often while he's working.
5 It's a profession for people who are ________.
6 It's very different from an ________ job.
7 The opinion of the ________ is important to James.
8 It's important to ________ the food.

6 Would you like to do James' job? Why / Why not? Write three or four sentences.

____

____

____

____

LANGUAGE IN ACTION

Future continuous and future perfect

1 Complete the sentences with the verbs in brackets in the future continuous.

1 I _'ll be reading_ (read) this book all evening.

2 He ______________ (listen) to the podcast later.

3 I ______________ (not lie) on the sofa all afternoon!

4 My parents ______________ (not work) this time tomorrow.

5 ______________ (we / eat) at two o'clock?

6 ______________ (Aidan / cook) for a long time?

2 Look at Chloe's diary. Complete the sentences with the correct future continuous form of the verbs in brackets and short or long answers.

Monday	Tuesday	Wednesday
tennis (5 pm)	homework (morning)	dance class (6 pm)

1 She _'ll be playing_ (play) tennis at 5 pm on Monday.

2 She ______________ (not do) homework on Tuesday afternoon.

3 She ______________ (start) her dance class at 6 pm on Wednesday.

4 A ______________ (Chloe / play tennis) on Monday?

B ______________

5 A What day ______________ (she / have) her dance class?

B ______________

3 Circle the correct options.

1 I'm going to bed very late tonight. I *'ll* / (*won't*) have gone to bed by 11 pm.

2 I hope that I *'ll* / *won't* have learned to drive in a few years' time. I think it would be fantastic!

3 My mum works abroad. By tomorrow, I *'ll* / *won't* have seen her for two months.

4 My dad often cooks for the family. He *'ll* / *won't* have cooked several meals for us by the end of this week.

5 A Will you have become a doctor by the time you're 20?

B That's impossible! *Yes, I will.* / *No, I won't.*

4 Complete the conversation with the verbs in the box in the future perfect and short answers.

arrive grill ~~make~~ not fry not have slice

A [1] _Will you have made_ (you) lunch by one o'clock?

B No, [2] ______________. Why?

A The guests [3] ______________ by then!

B Oh, no! I [4] ______________ the potatoes to make the chips, but I [5] ______________ them.

A And [6] ______________ (you) all the meat?

B No, [7] ______________. I [8] ______________ time!

5 Circle the correct time expression.

1 I'll be sleeping (*in two hours' time*) / *by the end of this week.*

2 Will you be sitting by the pool *this time tomorrow* / *by the time you're 18*?

3 We'll have finished all our exams *by the end of this month* / *for three hours*!

4 *Next Tuesday* / *By the end of this year,* we'll have visited five different countries!

5 We'll be eating that roast chicken *in five minutes* / *by the time it's cooked.*

6 Use the future continuous or future perfect to write about things that you will do / you hope that you will do.

1 By the end of this year, ______________.

2 At nine o'clock tonight, ______________.

3 Next weekend, ______________.

4 By the time I'm 30, ______________.

WRITING

A listicle

1 ☆ **Look at the listicle quickly. What is it about?**

____

2 ☆☆ **Read the listicle. Are the sentences *T* (true) or *F* (false)?**

1 Tight clothes will be popular. F

2 We will need to buy new clothes more often. ___

3 We will wear very different shoes from today. ___

4 We'll have less choice when we buy clothes. ___

5 Clothes will become intelligent. ___

3 ☆☆☆ **Rewrite the sentences with the <u>underlined</u> *Useful language phrases* in the listicle.**

1 More information here soon!

Watch this space!

2 Smart clothes will be the usual thing we wear.

____

3 I can't imagine anything more exciting than being a fashion designer.

____

4 T-shirts will always be popular. *(three expressions)*

____

FIVE FUTURE FASHION TRENDS!

1 Baggy clothes will be everywhere!

Comfortable baggy clothes <u>will be the norm</u> as the planet gets hotter. Tight denim jeans will have gone completely out of fashion by 2030, and clothes made of cool cotton will be in all the shops.

2 Clothes will wear out more quickly!

Fast fashion will mean that most clothes will only last five or six months. Clothes will become cheaper as a result.

3 Trainers <u>are here to stay</u>!

People of all ages wear trainers nowadays and that isn't going to change. If you ask me, trainers <u>will be around forever</u>. I love trainers, so <u>what could be better</u> news than that?

4 Clothes to match eyes and hair colour!

Very soon, we won't just be buying clothes by size. You'll be able to buy clothes to match your eyes or hair colour. Everything will be personalised. <u>Watch this space!</u>

5 High-tech clothes!

We already have smart phones and they <u>aren't going anywhere</u>. But soon we'll have smart clothes, too! They'll adapt to our body temperature and even to our size! The future's going to be exciting!

Write your own listicle.

PLAN

4 ☆☆ **Make notes on the theme 'Five ways my life will be different in 20 years' time'. Use the mind map to generate ideas.**

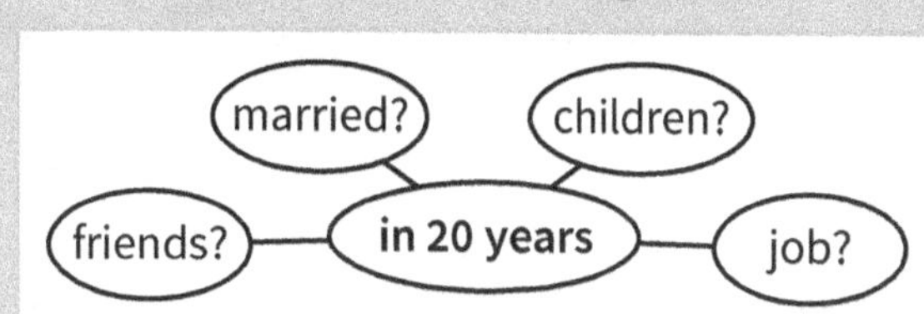

WRITE

5 ☆☆☆ **Write your listicle. Remember to include future tenses, vocabulary from this unit and expressions from the *Useful language* box (see Student's Book, p41).**

CHECK

6 **Do you ...**

- explain what you will or might be doing in the future?
- explain what will be normal in the future?
- make any other predictions?

3 REVIEW

VOCABULARY

1 Complete the crossword. Use the clues.

ACROSS →

4 ________ an egg
6 ________ an apple
7 ________ bread
8 ________ chicken
10 ________ a cake
11 ________ sausages

DOWN ↓

1 ________ onions
2 ________ a veggie burger
3 ________ cheese
5 ________ water
7 ________ meat
9 ________ butter

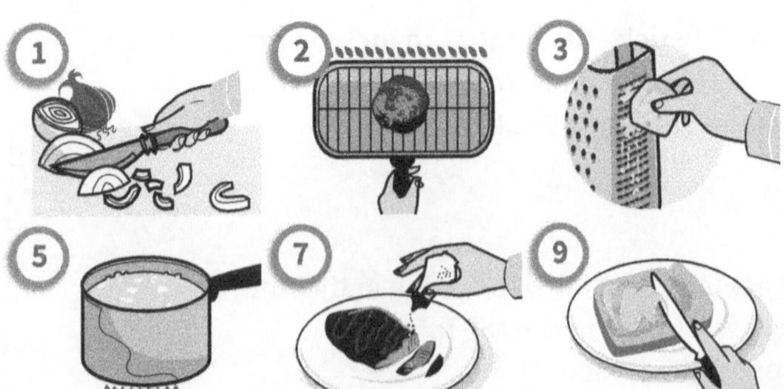

2 Circle the correct options.

1 a cup of *sugar* / *fish*
2 a piece of *salt* / *chocolate*
3 a slice of *cake* / *milk*
4 some chunks of *yoghurt* / *cheese*
5 a handful of *nuts* / *milk*
6 a packet of *water* / *crisps*
7 a pinch of *pepper* / *chicken*
8 a sprinkle of *potatoes* / *grated cheese*
9 a spoonful of *apples* / *olive oil*
10 a splash of *vinegar* / *salt*

LANGUAGE IN ACTION

3 Circle the correct options.

1 What time *does* / *will* the film start?
2 I *will* / *'m going to* make pizza for the first time next weekend.
3 *Do you go* / *Are you going* to the market with Sean this weekend?
4 Dad *might* / *will* be late for dinner tonight. It depends on when he finishes work.
5 I think that in the future people *will eat* / *are eating* less meat.
6 My cousin *will stay* / *is staying* at my house tonight.

4 Complete the predictions with the verbs in brackets in the future perfect or future continuous.

Space predictions

- In 20 years' time, scientists [1] ________ (discover) a new planet in our solar system.
- People [2] ________ (live) on Mars by the end of this century.
- A big asteroid [3] ________ (not hit) the Earth by the end of this millennium.
- People [4] ________ (go) to the moon for their holidays in 50 years' time.
- We [5] ________ (not find) intelligent life in the rest of the universe by the end of this century.
- Scientists [6] ________ (plan) journeys outside the solar system very soon.

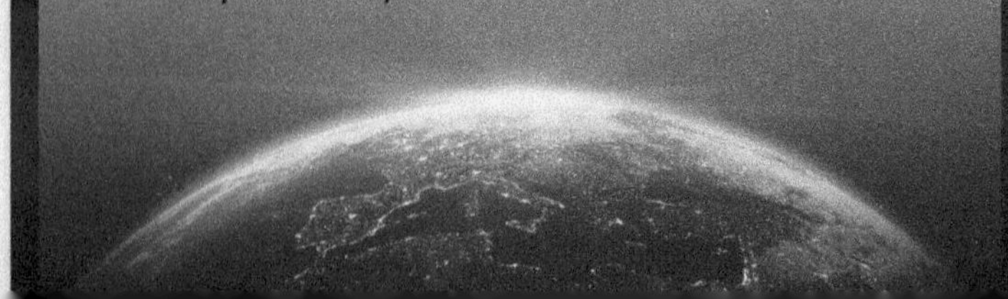

CUMULATIVE LANGUAGE

5 **Complete the text with the missing words. Circle the correct options.**

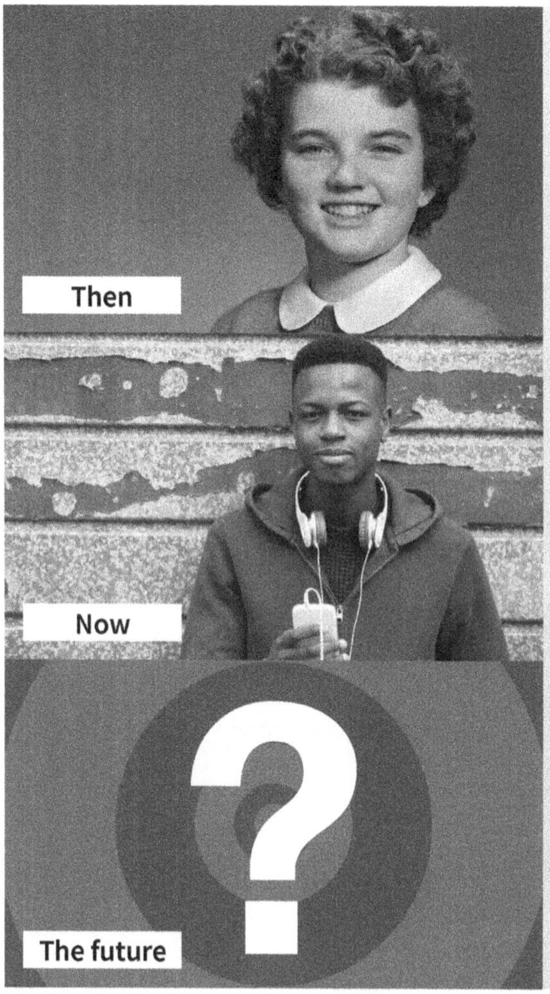

Teen fashion: past, present and future

Teenagers [1] ________ clothes especially designed for them for long. Before the 1950s, they [2] ________ their own fashion, and clothes companies [3] ________ about making special clothes for them. In the past, young teenagers [4] ________ children's clothes and teenagers that were [5] ________ older wore adult's clothes. Clothes for teenagers [6] ________ a lot since then! It's [7] ________ hard to predict what kind of clothes teenagers [8] ________ in the future because fashion changes very quickly. They [9] ________ wear high-tech clothes or perhaps they [10] ________ 1960s hippy-style clothes soon. Who knows? Two things are [11] ________ clear though – fashion designers [12] ________ very good at inventing new teen styles in the past and they [13] ________ to continue doing this in the future, too.

1 a weren't wearing b haven't been wearing c haven't worn
2 a didn't use to have b wouldn't have c weren't having
3 a have never thought b would never think c had never thought
4 a have been wearing b would wear c were wearing
5 a a bit b really c a far
6 a had changed b have changed c have been changing
7 a extremely b a lot c absolutely
8 a are wearing b will have worn c will be wearing
9 a will b might c 're going to
10 a wear b 're wearing c 'll be wearing
11 a pretty b a lot c far
12 a are b have been c had been
13 a are trying b will have tried c are going to try

4 SENSE AND SENSITIVITY

VOCABULARY

The five senses

a

b

c

d
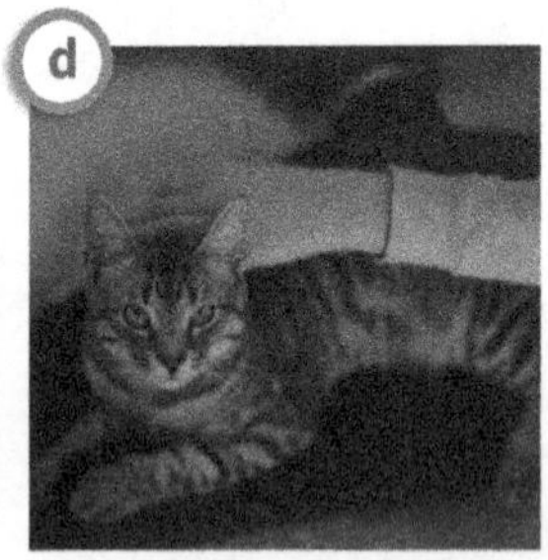

e

1 ★ **Match the sentences (1–5) with the pictures (A–E).**

1 It sounds good. [E]
2 It looks amazing! [ ]
3 It smells good. [ ]
4 It feels nice. [ ]
5 It tastes great. [ ]

2 ★★ **Complete the sentences with the correct form of *feel*, *look*, *smell*, *sound* or *taste* and *like*, if necessary.**

1 That song _sounds_ good. Who is it?
2 I love this ice cream. It ________ fantastic!
3 You ________ a film star in those sunglasses!
4 Can you give me a massage? Ah, that ________ so good!
5 Please open the window. It doesn't ________ good in here!
6 Do I ________ an English person when I speak English?
7 This bread ________ cardboard! It's very dry!
8 The sky ________ dark. I think it's going to rain.

3 ★★ **Complete the table with your own ideas. Write three things for each column. (see the *Learn to learn* tip in the Student's Book, p47.)**

It feels good	It looks good	It smells good	It sounds good	It tastes good
A cat's fur				

4 ★★★ **Write four sentences about what you experienced with your senses yesterday. Use *feel*, *look*, *smell*, *sound* or *taste* (*like*).**

My new shoes looked good.
____
____
____
____

Explore it!

Guess the correct answer.
How far away can elephants smell water?
a 5 km b 12 km c 19 km

Find another interesting fact about animal senses and email the question to a classmate or ask them in the next class.

THE BEST JOB IN THE WORLD?

HOME | **STORIES** | PHOTOS

For most of us, eating chocolate is a pleasure. But for Alice Schaffer, it's much more than that – it's a full-time job! Alice, you see, works for an important food company and she eats their chocolate to see how it tastes. Before she worked there, she didn't have a **background** in food science. She was, in fact, working as a secretary. Then one day a neighbour told her that her company was looking for people to work as taste-testers. Alice immediately thought, 'That sounds like a great job! And I might be good at it because I love chocolate!' So she applied and … they gave her the job! Of course, it isn't enough to like chocolate if you want to get a job tasting chocolate. You need to be able to identify and **accurately** describe different **flavours** and textures. And that's something you can't learn – you're either born with it or you aren't.

When Alice tells people what she **does for a living**, they often look surprised because they imagine that she must spend all day eating chocolate. But her job isn't really like that at all. When she tastes the chocolate from a bar, she just eats a little piece. You don't need to eat the whole bar to know what it tastes like! The hardest part of the job is when she tastes something that isn't 100% right. The **challenge** is to describe exactly what's wrong with the taste. The food technicians need this precise information so they can investigate the problem.

Alice is extremely **proud** of her job, and it's easy to see why: there can't be many people in the world whose job helps to give so much pleasure to others!

READING

A magazine article

1 Look at the text quickly. What is Alice Schaffer's job?

a She makes chocolate.
b She checks the taste of chocolate.
c She works in a chocolate factory.

2 Match the words in bold in the article with the definitions.

1 feeling pleasure because you've done something well ___proud___
2 how food or drink tastes ______
3 someone's past situation ______
4 correctly, without making any mistakes ______
5 do to earn money ______
6 something that needs effort, that might be hard to do ______

3 Read the text again. For each question, circle the correct option.

1 What is the writer trying to do in this article?
  a Explain how to get a job as a chocolate taster.
  b Write a biography of Alice Schaffer.
  c Describe what a chocolate taster does.
  d Tell the reader about the professional life of Alice Schaffer.
2 What kind of useful experience had Alice had before?
  a She had worked as a secretary.
  b She had studied food science.
  c She hadn't really had any experience.
  d Her neighbour had taught her about the job.
3 What is the principal quality you need to be a chocolate taster?
  a dedication b natural talent c to love chocolate d to write very well
4 What is the most difficult part of the job?
  a Giving precise information when the quality isn't good.
  b Not eating the chocolate.
  c Some people don't think it's a serious job.
  d Working with the food technicians.
5 What might Alice say to a friend about her job?
  a It's an easy job.
  b I love my job!
  c There's often a lot of stress in my job.
  d The chocolate is bad for me.

4 Would you like to do Alice Schaffer's job? Why / Why not?

______

______

______

LANGUAGE IN ACTION

Deduction and possibility

1 ★ **Match the sentences (1–3) with their meanings (a–c).**

1 I'm sure it's nice to work as a chocolate taster. ☐
2 Perhaps it's nice to work as a chocolate taster. ☐
3 I'm sure it isn't nice to work as a chocolate taster. ☐

a It can't be nice to work as a chocolate taster.
b It must be nice to work as a chocolate taster.
c It might be nice to work as a chocolate taster.

2 ★★ **Look at the sentence *It might be nice to work as a chocolate taster.* Which two modal verbs with the same meaning can we use in place of *might*?**

____

3 ★ **Circle the correct options to describe the pictures.**

1 He *can't* / *must* be tired.

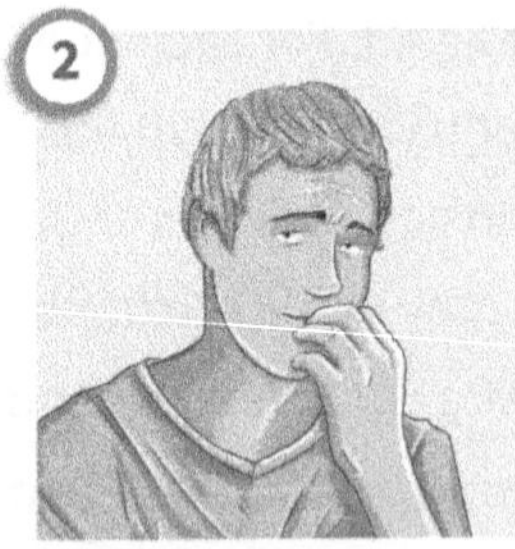

2 He *can't* / *must* feel relaxed.

3 That car *can't* / *must* be expensive!

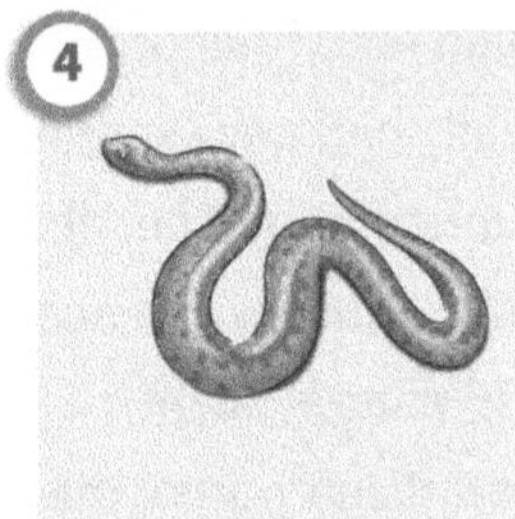

4 Careful! It *might* / *must* be dangerous

5 It *can't* / *must* be raining.

6 They *might* / *can't* still have some good bargains.

4 ★★ **Complete the conversation about the photo with *must*, *might* or *can't*.**

A Look at this photo! What is it?
B It [1] might be a house!
A No, it [2] ______ be! How would you get in?
B It [3] ______ be a fake photo. You never know …
A No, the photo's real. I think it [4] ______ be art or something. There [5] ______ be another explanation. I'm sure the artist is famous.
B Perhaps …, you [6] ______ be right. The person who designed it [7] ______ be very creative!!

5 ★★★ **Rewrite the sentences so that they have the same meaning. Use *must*, *might*, *could* or *can't*.**

1 Perhaps Nathan's still at school.
Nathan might/could still be at school.
2 I'm sure that isn't the right answer.
____
3 I'm sure you need good exam results to do medicine at university.
____
4 This is possibly the worst film I've seen!
____
5 I'm sure it doesn't take a long time to make that dish.
____

6 ★★★ **Write deductions about these situations. Use *must*, *might* or *can't*.**

1 Matt is a professional footballer.
He must be very fit.
2 All the shops are closed.
____
3 Your mobile phone isn't working.
____
4 Everyone is looking at the sky.
____

VOCABULARY AND LISTENING

Describing texture, sound, taste, etc.

1 ☆ **Complete the adjectives.**

1 spic y
2 rou __ __
3 shin __
4 fain __
5 colour __ __ __ __
6 sou __
7 smoo __ __
8 shar __
9 smell __

2 ☆☆ **Write an appropriate adjective from Exercise 1 before the nouns.**

1 spicy curry
2 dirty, ________ socks
3 nice, ________ skin
4 ________ cream
5 ________, new scissors
6 ________ flowers

3 ☆☆ **Complete the sentences with adjectives from Exercise 1.**

1 A crocodile has very sharp teeth.
2 This sauce is too ________ for me. My mouth's burning!
3 Can you pass the sugar? This yoghurt is very ________.
4 Does this cake have bananas in it? I can detect a ________ taste of them, but it's not very strong.
5 This cream is great! My hands feel so ________!
6 This metal box looks very ________ when it's in the sun.
7 Tom's chin felt ________ because he hadn't shaved.

4 ☆☆☆ **Write short descriptions of the items in the box. Use at least one adjective from Exercise 1 in each description. You can use affirmative or negative verbs.**

apple	cats	my favourite food	snakes

1 ________
2 ________
3 ________
4 ________

An interview

5 4.01 ☆ **Listen to an interview about the senses. According to Simon Redding, which of our senses is the most important?**

a hearing ☐
b sight ☐
c smell ☐
d touch ☐

6 4.01 ☆☆ **Listen again. For each question, circle the correct option.**

1 Simon says that some people …
 (a) can't smell very much.
 b use sight and smell well.
 c feel cold all the time.
2 What does Simon say about dreams?
 a Some people open their eyes when they dream.
 b It's good to have colourful images.
 c Taste and smell are not usually part of dreams.
3 When we are communicating, we …
 a shouldn't only be listening.
 b need to smile.
 c shouldn't be negative.
4 What has the biggest impact on us in a conversation?
 a What the other person expresses without words.
 b How the other person moves and looks at us.
 c The language which the other person uses.
5 What would Simon Redding like people to do?
 a To depend on their eyes to understand better
 b To remember to use all of their senses
 c To close their eyes and feel objects

7 ☆☆☆ **Think about what you have done today. When have you used each of the five senses?**

____
____
____
____

LANGUAGE IN ACTION

Obligation, prohibition, necessity and advice

1 ★★ **(Circle) the correct options.**

How to use music to relax

- You [1](should) / *don't need to* listen to calm music.
- You [2]*don't have to* / *mustn't* listen to heavy metal. It's not relaxing!
- You [3]*ought to* / *shouldn't* sit in a comfortable position.
- You [4]*need to* / *mustn't* concentrate on the music.
- To help you concentrate, you [5]*don't need to* / *should* close your eyes.
- You [6]*shouldn't* / *don't need to* be with other people when you listen to the music. It's far better if you are alone.
- You [7]*mustn't* / *don't need to* wear headphones, but it's better if you have them.

2 ★★ **Complete the interview with a perfume maker with the missing words. (Circle) the correct options.**

A [1]________ study a lot before you became a perfume maker?

B Yes, I [2]________ I [3]________ study chemistry for four years.

A And I suppose that a perfume maker [4]________ to have a good sense of smell!

B Yes, of course. You [5]________ consider becoming a perfume maker without that! And you [6]________ to be very patient because it takes a long time to create the right smell. And you [7]________ copy other people. That's bad! You [8]________ to be original!

	a	b	c
1	Must you	Should you	(c) Did you have to
2	must	have	did
3	had to	need to	ought to
4	must	should	needs
5	should	shouldn't	don't have to
6	must	need	don't have
7	mustn't	don't need to	should
8	must	have	should

3 ★★★ **Rewrite the sentences with *must*, *should*, *need* or *have to*.**

1 I recommend that you see a doctor.
You should see a doctor.

2 It's not permitted to walk on the grass.

3 There's no obligation for us to watch the match.

4 Jack didn't have an obligation to give me a present.

5 It's necessary for us to contact him.

6 Being in the sun without a hat is not recommended.

4 ★★★ **Answer the questions so they are true for you.**

1 What do you need to do today?

2 What did you have to do yesterday?

3 What mustn't you do at school?

4 What should you do but you sometimes don't?

WRITING

An encyclopaedia entry

Marlee Matlin, 24 August 1965

1 Marlee Matlin is an actress. She is the only deaf actress who has won an Oscar.

2 Marlee was born in 1965 and grew up in a small town near Chicago. At the age of 18 months, she lost almost all her hearing. She acted for the first time at the age of seven in a production of *The Wizard of Oz* with actors who were all deaf. In 1986, she won the Oscar for best actress at the age of only 21. In the film she didn't have to speak. She played the role of a deaf woman who refuses to speak because the rest of the world refuses to learn sign language.

3 Marlee has appeared in many films and TV shows, including *Sesame Street*. She isn't just famous as an actress; she is also known as an enthusiastic worker for many charities.

4 Marlee can speak quite well, and she doesn't always need to use an interpreter because she can read people's lips. According to her autobiography, she never planned to become an actress. She thought there wouldn't be any opportunities for deaf people.

1 **Read the encyclopaedia entry. Which of Marlee's senses is damaged?**

____

2 **Complete the sentences with information from the encyclopaedia entry.**

1 She was born _in 1965_.
2 When she was seven, ________.
3 In the film where she won an Oscar, her character was ________.
4 She is also famous as ________.
5 She can read people's lips, so ________.
6 When she was young, she used to think that ________.

3 **Complete the sentences with the underlined *Useful language* in the encyclopaedia entry.**

Javier Bardem [1] _grew up_ in Madrid but he [2] ______ in Las Palmas in the Canary Islands. In his career he has acted in many movies [3] ______ *Skyfall*, a James Bond film. He actually appeared in his first film [4] ______ only six. [5] ______ Bardem, he originally wanted to be a painter, but he didn't have enough talent. Outside films, Bardem is ` [6] ______ a firm defender of ecological causes.

Write an encyclopaedia entry:

PLAN

4 **Write notes in your notebook about your favourite actor, fictional character or sportsperson.**

- Name and date of birth
- A short general description
- Information about their life
- An interesting fact

WRITE

5 **Write your entry. Remember to include four paragraphs, some modal verbs, vocabulary from this unit and expressions from the *Useful language* box (see Student's Book, p53).**

CHECK

6 **Do you …**

- include a title?
- include information about the person's life and achievements?
- include an interesting fact?

4 REVIEW

VOCABULARY

1 Complete the sentences with the correct form of *feel* (*like*), *look* (*like*), *smell* (*like*), *sound* (*like*) or *taste* (*like*).

1 It doesn't ________ very good in here. Please open the windows.

2 When you sing, you don't really ________ an angel!

3 Wow! That photo ________ a painting! It's so artistic!

4 A Do you want to go skateboarding?
B Yes, that ________ a good idea!

5 This perfume ________ roses and oranges. It's great!

6 It ________ an oven in here! Please put the air conditioning on!

7 This strawberry ice cream ________ great! Did you make it yourself?

8 These tomatoes ________ quite green and they ________ really hard. So, I don't think they're going to ________ very nice!

2 Complete the crossword. Use the clues.

Down ↓

1 That jumper is ________. You need to wash it.

2 I like the feel of this leather. It's very ________.

4 There's a ________ taste of lemon in this cake but it isn't very strong.

5 Be careful – it's very ________! Don't cut yourself!

Across →

1 If you have a stomach ache, you shouldn't eat ________ food.

2 I love Chinese food, especially sweet and ________ chicken.

3 That bird is very ________. It looks beautiful.

5 The metal buttons on your coat look very ________ under these lights.

6 A rhinoceros has hard, ________ skin.

LANGUAGE IN ACTION

3 Complete the conversation with *might*, *must* or *can't*.

A Is the new *Mission Impossible* film good?

B I haven't seen it yet, but it [1] ________ be pretty good. It's got four stars in the newspaper.

A You never know, it [2] ________ be awful.

B You [3] ________ be serious! They spend a lot of money to make those films. So, it [4] ________ be fantastic!

A Hmm, you [5] ________ be right. But it [6] ________ be as good as the last one. That's the best film I've ever seen.

B You [7] ________ be surprised. David's seen it and he couldn't stop talking about it!

A Really? Then it [8] ________ be great! David and I always agree about films!

4 **Complete the sentences with the correct form of *must*, (*don't*) *need to*, *should* or (*don't*) *have to*.**

1 You ___________ touch the paintings. It's not allowed!
2 We ___________ get up early this morning because the train left at seven o'clock.
3 I don't think you ___________ wear green with purple, but it's your decision.
4 I ___________ borrow your bike, but thanks for the offer.
5 ___________ (you) ___________ wear a uniform at your old school?
6 I ___________ tidy my bedroom tonight, but I'm not going to do it.
7 You ___________ help me, but it'd be great if you could.
8 ___________ (we) get a visa to travel to Turkey?

CUMULATIVE LANGUAGE

5 **Complete the conversation with the missing words. Circle the correct options.**

CHRIS What [1] ___________ this weekend?
TOM I [2] ___________ any plans yet.
CHRIS What about this new Sensorium exhibition? It [3] ___________ be good. You never know.
TOM I [4] ___________! It was so interesting that I [5] ___________ about it all the time. It [6] ___________ be the best exhibition I've ever been to. I'm [7] ___________ sure of that. I [8] ___________ that going to museums to look at paintings was boring. But this exhibition is different because you listen to music and smell things while you're looking at each painting. I [9] ___________ that an exhibition could be like that! You [10] ___________ go, Chris! You [11] ___________ disappointed!
CHRIS Thanks! I [12] ___________ miss it! By next Monday both of us [13] ___________ it!

	a	b	c
1	do you do	will you do	are you doing
2	didn't make	haven't made	haven't been making
3	might	must	will
4	'd already been	already went	've already been
5	've been thinking	've thought	think
6	can	needs to	must
7	rather	absolutely	far
8	would think	used to think	've been thinking
9	've never imagined	might never imagine	'd never imagined
10	should	don't have to	'll
11	can't be	won't be	haven't been
12	won't	don't need to	aren't going to
13	will see	will have seen	will be seeing

EXAM TIPS: Listening skills

Listening Part 1: Multiple-choice pictures

You will listen to short extracts and choose from different options. This exam task tests your ability to listen for specific information and answer questions about what you hear.

Exam guide: Multiple choice

- If the question is about a dialogue between a boy and a girl, underline which of the two people you need to answer the question about. For example: *What food will the boy eat?*
- Decide if the question is asking about the past, present or future. The verb tense and time expressions in the question will help you. For example: *What is the weather like now?* is a completely different question from: *What will the weather be like tomorrow?*
- Listen carefully to see if the meaning is positive or negative. For example: *Can you buy some fruit – but not bananas?* tells us that the speaker does not want bananas.
- Usually the answer will come in the middle or at the end of the listening and not at the beginning. This means that you should always wait until the end of each listening before you choose your answer.

REMEMBER!

Don't choose a picture as an answer just because you hear information about it in the listening. Usually you will hear information related to all three pictures!

Listening practice: Multiple-choice pictures

Tip!

Listen for key words or synonyms to help you identify the answer.

1 Choose the correct meaning for the expressions.

1 Are you kidding me?
  A I don't believe you. B That's interesting!
2 You're getting on my nerves.
  A You're funny! B You're irritating me!
3 You'll never know unless you try.
  A You should try. B Are you going to try?
4 You're coming to my party, aren't you?
  A Are you sure you're coming to my party?
  B Can you confirm that you're coming to my party?
5 You must feel really proud of your exam results!
  A I'm sure you feel really happy about your exam results.
  B You ought to feel very happy about your exam results.
6 I get a lot out of playing chess.
  A Playing chess is hard for me. B I really enjoy playing chess.

2 E.01 **You will hear six short extracts. Are the sentences *T* (true) or *F* (false)?**

1 The boy's sister irritates the girl. ___
2 The speaker says everyone should study abroad. ___
3 The boy's coffee is very hot. ___
4 There is a present in the box. ___
5 Some fruit tastes better than it smells. ___
6 The girl thinks going to university is a bad idea. ___

Tip!

Sometimes information later in the listening will contradict or correct the information before. For example:
A: *Amy loves skateboarding.*
B: *Well, that was before her accident. She hasn't done it since then.*
This is another reason why you need to wait till the end before choosing your answer.

3 E.02 **Listen to the conversation between Ben and his mum. Answer *Yes* or *No*.**

1 Are the dishes washed? ___
2 Does Ben need to do his homework tonight? ___
3 Is Ben going to speak to his friends tonight? ___

4 E.02 **Listen again. What is Ben going to do first? Choose the correct option A, B or C.**

A

B

C

EXAM TIPS: Reading skills

Reading Part 2: Multiple matching

Matching people with activities and things

You will read descriptions of people and match them with the best options. Remember that there may be more options than people, so read carefully! The extra options usually fit only partially, not completely.

Exam guide: Multiple matching

- Begin by reading the five descriptions of the people. Underline the key information in each description.
- Next, read all eight texts carefully and underline the key information in each one.
- Then compare the underlined information in the description of the first person with the underlined information in the texts. Which text is the best match for this person?
- Don't choose a text just because it repeats some words from the description of one person. You need to focus on the meaning of the descriptions and the texts and not on individual words.

REMEMBER!

Be very careful when choosing – the text needs to be a perfect match for everything the person wants.

Reading practice: Multiple matching

Identifying meaning

1 Choose the option (A, B or C) that shows the meaning of the first sentence.

1 Jack wants to do without chocolate for a week.
  A Jacks wants to eat less chocolate for a week.
  B Jack thinks he can do without chocolate for a week.
  C Jack would like not to eat chocolate for seven days.

2 Chloe is looking forward to learning to drive.
  A Chloe plans to learn to drive.
  B Chloe is happy that she will start driving soon.
  C In the future Chloe will learn to drive.

3 Liam has moved to Liverpool.
  A Liam is living in Liverpool now.
  B Liam has travelled to Liverpool.
  C Liam is spending some time in Liverpool.

Synonyms

2 Match the underlined words with the synonyms in the box. There are four extra words.

be born	can	cook in oil	cook in the oven	cut into pieces
heat	know	lived as a child	think	will possibly

1 I'm going to bake a cake. ________
2 Jon grew up in Chicago. ________
3 How long does it take to fry the onions? ________
4 Rachel might go to university. ________
5 I guess they must be brother and sister. ________
6 You need to chop the peppers. ________

Tip!
Don't look for words that match exactly. Read the text carefully and underline synonyms of the key information words.

Eliminating options

3 Read what Laura wants. Then decide which option(s) (A–D) you can eliminate.

Laura wants to buy a new mobile phone. It must be the latest model, transparent, feel very light and smooth and have a very large display.

A We repair all the latest models of mobile phones …
B Our shop has a good selection of mobile phones, including classic old models …
C We have the latest models. They're transparent, very light and have big displays. We're definitely the best place to get a new watch.
D This shop specialises in all sorts of digital devices. Its products are expensive, but they look great!

Tip!
When you think you have a correct answer, check the incorrect options again to be sure that they don't match.

Finding differences

4 Read about Sam and Nathan. Find three differences between them.

Sam wants to try out some new recipes. He cooks every day. During the week he hasn't got much time to cook, but he's got time at the weekend to make more complicated dishes. He doesn't eat fried food or food with a very strong flavour.

Nathan likes very spicy food. He wants to buy a book of recipes. He is especially interested in making quick meals in the frying pan.

____
____
____

EXAM TIPS: Listening skills

Listening Part 3: Gap-fill

In this part of the exam, you have to listen and complete notes or sentences. The notes or sentences summarise what you hear. You have to write a word, number or a very short noun phrase.

Exam guide: Gap-fill

- Pay attention to the instructions. They remind you what you have to do, but more importantly, they tell you what the topic is.
- After the instructions there is a pause. Use this to read the notes or sentences.
- While you read, try to think about what type of word is missing. It might be a day, a number, a date or price, for example.
- The sentences or notes summarise what the speaker says so you are not going to hear what is written on the page. Pay attention to the key words.
- As you listen, write down the words – remember the answers are one word or a very short phrase.
- During the second listening, check your answers.

REMEMBER!

Check that your answers make sense in the context if you are given a second opportunity to listen.

Tip!

The sentences and notes will give you clues about what type of information is missing. Read everything carefully.

LISTENING PRACTICE: Gap-fill

1 **Read the notes. What type of information is missing?**

Hire a bus
Number of seats on our bus: 1 ________
Bus leaves: 10.30 am
Meet at youth club: 2 ________
Price of exhibition entrance: £5
Special group price (over 20 people): 3 £________

2 E.03 **You will hear some information about a visit to a photography exhibition. Listen and write the correct answer in the gaps (1–3) in Exercise 1. Then, listen again and write down the other numbers that you hear.**

____

Tip!

What you read in the exam questions is not what the person says – it is a summary or paraphrase. Think about the meaning and listen for key words.

3 E.04 **Listen and complete the sentences.**

A Angela's mum told her that her __________ had won the competition many years ago.

B To find out more about the competition, visit the website – www.__________.org.

C Angela entered the competition with her __________.

D The class was given a grant of £ __________ to build their robot.

4 **You will hear an announcement about events coming up at a youth club. Before you listen, read the notes in Exercise 5. What type of information is missing from the gaps?**

a type of clothing | day | name of food | number | subject | time

5 E.05 **Listen and complete the notes with one or two words or a number or a date or a time.**

Youth club events: November

Weekly cooking classes:

Every [1] __________ at 5 pm

Mary

1) bake a chocolate cake; 2) roast [2] __________

Visit 1:

Date: Friday 16th at [3] __________ pm

Helen Fields – fashion designer

Workshop: match colours; choose jeans; decorate a plain white [4] __________ (must bring)

Visit 2:

Date: Saturday, 24th at 7 pm

Dr Michael Redding – Professor of [5] __________

Talk: history of logos

Logo competition:

1st prize [6] £__________ in cash

LANGUAGE REFERENCE

Present and past simple and continuous

- We use the **present simple** to talk about facts, habits and routines.
  My sister likes pizza.
  I don't read every day.
- We use the **past simple** to talk about completed events and actions in the past.
  I translated the text into Spanish for him.
  I visited Madrid three years ago.
- We use the **present continuous** to talk about actions that are happening now or around now.
  That girl over there is waving at me.
- We use the **past continuous** to talk about actions in progress around a time in the past. We also use ***when***, ***while*** and ***as*** to mean 'during that time' or to connect two events happening at the same time.
  Isabella was wearing a dress last night.
  While I was looking for the dog, he was looking for the ball.

Present perfect and past simple

- We use the **present perfect** when something started or happened in the past and continues to be true until now. We can say how long something has been true, but not when it started.
  I've been to Barcelona. (when isn't specified, but it continues to be true)
  They've been sightseeing. (we don't know when)
  She's wanted to shake your hand since she arrived. (she continues to want to)
- We use the **past simple** when the moment in which something happened has ended. When it happened isn't always mentioned, usually because it is clear.
  I went to Barcelona in June.
  They went sightseeing yesterday.
  She wanted to shake your hand.

LANGUAGE PRACTICE

Present and past simple and continuous

1 Choose the correct options.

1 I (cut) / *was cutting* my finger yesterday.
2 *Do you go* / *Are you going* to the supermarket now?
3 What *happens* / *is happening* when you push this button?
4 Mary *listened* / *was listening* to music when I *saw* / *was seeing* her.
5 You *don't need* / *aren't needing* to pack a lot of clothes.
6 *Did you buy* / *Were you buying* some bread for a sandwich?

2 Complete the conversation with the correct form of the verbs in brackets.

MUM Harry, you're going to be late. What [1] are you doing (you / do)?
HARRY I [2] ________ (try) to find my keys!
MUM Where [3] ________ (you / normally / leave) them?
HARRY I always [4] ________ (put) them on my desk. But they're not there now.
MUM When [5] ________ (you / have) them last?
HARRY I [6] ________ (have) them in my hand when I [7] ________ (arrive) home yesterday. I [8] ________ (talk) to Jonah on the phone.
MUM Oh yes, I [9] ________ (remember). You [10] ________ (go) into the living room.
HARRY I [11] ________ (look) there, but I [12] ________ (not find) them.
MUM [13] ________ (you / wear) your coat?
HARRY Yes, I was. Maybe I [14] ________ (leave) them in my coat pocket. Here they are!

Present perfect and past simple

3 Complete the sentences with the present perfect or past simple form of the verbs in the box.

not laugh	not play	paint	~~see~~	sing	tell

1 Have you seen Scarlett? She's looking for you.
2 Pete ________ very well at the concert yesterday.
3 I ________ you 100 times! Don't call me Timmy!
4 Don't touch the door. They ________ just ________ it.
5 Why ________ you ________ at that joke? It was really funny.
6 Lucas ________ football for a month. He's injured.

4 Put the words in the correct order to make sentences.

1 sent / Has / photo / you / Erin / the ?
Has Erin sent you the photo?
2 tennis / I / liked / you / didn't / know / playing
____
3 long / your / taken / a / You / time / to / essay / have / finish
____
4 questions / the / didn't / exam / all / answer / in / the / We
____
5 you / us / did / Why / come / with / to / decide / ?
____
6 heard / from / We / news / Julia / any / haven't
____

LANGUAGE REFERENCE

Present perfect simple

- We use the **present perfect** to talk about actions, experiences and facts in the past, when the exact time is not mentioned or important.
  I've found my favourite T-shirt.
  She has been to the shops.

Present perfect continuous

	Affirmative	Negative
He / She / It	has been practising for years.	hasn't been eating very well.
I / We / You / They	have been practising for years.	haven't been eating very well.

Questions		
Has	he / she / it	been sleeping a lot?
Have	I / we / you / they	

Short answers		
Yes,	he / she / it	has.
	I / we / you / they	have.
No,	he / she / it	hasn't.
	I / we / you / they	haven't.

- We use the **present perfect continuous** to talk about an action or a series of actions that started in the past, is still in progress and we expect to continue.
  I've been studying hard all week.
  She's been exercising since last summer.
- We often use the **present perfect continuous** to say how long we have been doing something.
  I've been going to piano lessons for nine years.
- We use the **present perfect continuous** to focus on the ongoing action, rather than the result.
  We've been preparing for the party all day!
- We don't use the **present perfect continuous** with stative verbs (e.g. *like*, *have* and *know*).
  Emily has liked him since she met him.
  ~~*Emily has been liking him since she met him.*~~
  We have had our cat since she was a kitten.
  ~~*We've been having our cat since she was a kitten.*~~
- We form the **present perfect continuous** with **subject** + ***has/have*** **(*not*)** + ***been*** + ***-ing***.
  I've been playing basketball since I was seven.
  She's ill, so she hasn't been coming to school this week.
- We form **present perfect continuous** questions with ***has/have*** + **subject** + ***been*** + ***-ing***.
  Has she been living here for a long time?

Present perfect simple and present perfect continuous

- We use the **present perfect simple** to emphasise that the action or event is recently finished. The **present perfect continuous** is used for actions or events that are still going on up to now.
  I've studied for my English test tomorrow. (completed action)
  I've been studying for my English test tomorrow. (ongoing)

Modifiers

- We use **modifiers** with adjectives to make the meaning stronger and show emphasis. Common modifiers include *a bit*, *much too*, *totally*, *really*, *absolutely*, *extremely*, *quite* and *rather*.
  He was really upset. I felt extremely sorry for him.
  Her parents are quite strict. She can't do anything.
  They work much too hard. They need to relax.
  Her room is really messy. There's stuff everywhere!

LANGUAGE PRACTICE

Present perfect simple

1 Complete the sentences with the present perfect simple form of the verbs in brackets.

1 I haven't worn (not wear) this dress since last spring!
2 Paul ______ (wait) all his life for this moment.
3 ______ Jane ______ (tell) you what happened yesterday?
4 We ______ (not play) this computer game for months.
5 Our school ______ (organise) a fashion show.

Present perfect continuous

2 Complete the sentences with the present perfect continuous form of the verbs in the box.

~~listen~~ rain run tidy wear

1 I 've been listening to this great radio station on my phone.
2 Your face is red. ______ you ______?
3 It ______ all morning, so we can't go out.
4 Her feet hurt because she ______ those high-heeled boots all day.
5 Vanessa ______ her room all morning – it was a terrible mess!

Present perfect simple and present perfect continuous

3 Circle the correct options.

1 How many times have you (seen) / *been seeing* this film?
2 I've *folded* / *been folding* all my clothes and they're in my suitcase now.
3 Have you *sent* / *been sending* the photos to me yet?
4 Dad's tired because he has *painted* / *been painting* all day.
5 Daniel hasn't *read* / *been reading* Laura's message yet, so don't tell him what she said.
6 I've *ordered* / *been ordering* pizzas – they'll be here in a few minutes.

4 Complete the conversation with the present perfect simple or continuous form of the verbs in brackets.

TIM Hi, Mia. I [1] haven't seen (not see) you all day. What [2] ______ (you / do)?

MIA Oh, hi Tim. I [3] ______ (study) for an exam. It's history. I [4] ______ (always / find) it hard to study history.

TIM Me too. I [5] ______ (even / not start) yet. I [6] ______ (try) to write that essay for English class. I [7] ______ (not finish) it yet though.

MIA I have. Do you want to see it? I [8] ______ (write) about my last holiday. I'm quite happy with it.

TIM That's funny. I [9] ______ (do) the same thing. Maybe the teacher's going to think we [10] ______ (copy) from each other!

Modifiers

5 Circle the correct options.

1 I'm not buying these trousers. They're *absolutely* / (*much too*) big for me.
2 The film was *really* / *totally* good and *a bit* / *quite* funny.
3 Lydia's dress was *totally* / *a lot* amazing, and her brother looked *rather* / *a little* handsome.
4 These jeans are *a bit* / *pretty* shorter than those ones.

6 Match the beginnings of the sentences with the ends.

1 The exam was really — e
2 I'm really
3 Yusuf thought the story was rather
4 Emir's party was a lot more
5 Liam takes totally amazing
6 The food was pretty

a fun than Carl's one last month.
b good, but I didn't like the music.
c sorry, but I can't talk now.
d amusing, but nobody else liked it.
e difficult, but I think I passed.
f photos, but he never shares them.

LANGUAGE REFERENCE

used to, *would* and past simple

- ***Used to*** emphasises that past states, habits and actions are now finished.
  It used to be a castle, but now it's a museum.
  She used to play piano. Today, she just sings.
- ***Used to*** does not have a present form. For present habits and states, we use the present simple.
  My cousin visits us every summer.
  ~~*My cousin use to visit us every summer.*~~
- We use ***used to*** and ***would*** to talk about habits and actions in the past that are different today.
  They used to run on Tuesdays, but now they run on Fridays.
  When I was young, my parents would take me for a walk every day.
- We also use ***used to***, but not ***would***, to talk about states and feelings in the past that are different today.
  My grandfather used to have black hair, but now it's white.
  ~~*My grandfather would have black hair …*~~
  She used to love volleyball, but she doesn't play anymore.
  ~~*She would love volleyball …*~~
- We do not use ***used to*** or ***would*** to talk about things that only happened once, or to say how many times something happened.
  Last year, I went to Mexico.
  ~~*Last year, I used to go to Mexico.*~~
  Yesterday, I called my dad three times.
  ~~*Yesterday, I would call dad three times.*~~
- We put question words at the beginning of the question.
  What things did you use to do when you were younger?
- We don't often use ***would*** in questions and negative sentences.
- ***Used to*** is like any regular verb. The past tense ends in ***d***, but in questions and negative forms, the verb does not end in ***d***.
  I used to like playing, but I didn't use to like practising.
  Did you use to have a bike when you were younger?

Past perfect with *never*, *already*, *by (then)*, *by the time*

- We use the **past perfect** with other past tenses to talk about actions or states that happened before the main past action or state.
  We hadn't seen the news, so we didn't know about the storms.
  I couldn't call you on Friday because I had left my phone at home.
- We use **adverbs** and **adverbial phrases** such as *already, ever, never, by the time* and *by then* with the past perfect.
- ***Already***, ***never*** and ***ever*** come before the past participle, but *yet* comes after.
  We had never been to New York until last year.
  They've gone to school, but they haven't had breakfast yet.
- We use ***already*** to emphasise that something had happened.
  I had already finished my test before class was over.
- If something had happened ***by the time*** something else happened, it happened before it.
  They had already heard the news when I told them.
- If something had happened ***by then***, it happened before then.
  I finally arrived at the party, but by then the food had all gone.

LANGUAGE PRACTICE

UNIT 2

used to, *would* and past simple

1 Complete the sentences with *used to* and the verbs in brackets.

1 I *didn't use to like* (not like) wearing dresses when I was younger.
2 Yuri ________ (eat) a lot of sweets until his dentist told him to stop.
3 Adela ________ (not look) forward to PE classes because she wasn't very fit.
4 Our football team ________ (win) every match, but now they're terrible!
5 My dad ________ (not have) a mobile phone when he was 15.
6 My teachers ________ (not give) us much homework.

2 Make questions with *used to* or the past simple. Sometimes both are possible.

1 When / Helen / buy / this car / ?
When did Helen buy this car?
2 there / always / be / a cinema here / ?
____
3 your dad / have / a bike / when he was a teenager / ?
____
4 you / hear / what happened yesterday / ?
____
5 What sort of music / you / listen to / when you were younger / ?
____

3 Choose the correct sentences. Sometimes both are correct.

1 (a) When she was younger, my aunt used to live in York.
b When she was younger, my aunt would live in York.
2 a When I was five, I wouldn't ever eat vegetables.
b When I was five, I didn't ever use to eat vegetables.
3 a There used to be a lot more shops in this street.
b There would be a lot more shops in this street.
4 a My dad used to have a long beard.
b My dad would have a long beard.

Past perfect with *never*, *already*, *by (then)*, *by the time*

4 Circle the correct options.

1 I was excited because I'd (never) / *already* been to a wedding before.
2 Had the teacher *already* / *never* started the class when Paul arrived?
3 By *then* / *the time* you called, it was too late to do anything.
4 When the film started they'd *never* / *already* eaten all the pizza.
5 I started running, but *by then* / *by the time* the man was too far away.
6 When we took my grandmother to Los Angeles, she had *never* / *ever* flown across the Atlantic before.

5 Complete the text with the words in the box.

already	by	had	had already	~~never~~	then

I was very nervous. I'd [1] *never* played the guitar in front of people before. I walked on to the stage. [2] ________ the time I'd picked up the guitar, my hands were shaking. They [3] ________ turned the lights off, so I couldn't really see much. I put the strap around my neck, but by [4] ________ the rest of the band had [5] ________ started playing the first song! I put my hands on the guitar to play … and there was no sound. Someone [6] ________ pulled the plug!

6 Use the prompts to make sentences in the past simple and past perfect.

1 They / not sleep / all night because / there / be / a big storm
They hadn't slept all night because there was a big storm.
2 By the time we / get / there, our team / score
____
3 She / try / to apologise to him the week before, but by then / it / be / too late
____
4 Until last week, Camilla / never / speak / in English
____
5 When you / arrive, Dennis / already / find / his keys
____

LANGUAGE REFERENCE

Future tenses

- We use ***be going to*** to talk about future plans and intentions and predictions that we feel sure about.
  After I graduate, I'm going to travel the world.
  My sister is going to stay with my grandparents this summer.
  I'm going to feel ill if I eat all of that!
- We use ***will*** to talk about what is going to happen in the future, especially things that you are certain about or things that are planned.
  I'll see him tomorrow.
  I won't cook later – I'll be out.
- We use ***may* (*not*)** or ***might* (*not*)** instead of ***will* (*not*)** to show that we feel less sure about a future action or event, but think it is probable.
  I might not go to university.
  I may get a job with my dad.
  When he gets here, he may want to speak to you.
  Don't call after ten o'clock – we may be watching a film.

Present continuous for future

- We use the **present continuous** to talk about future arrangements when the time is fixed.
  They're getting married this summer.
  What are you doing this weekend? – I'm going shopping with my parents.
  She isn't coming to the party. She's spending the day with her cousins.

Present simple for future

- We use the **present simple** to talk about events that are scheduled or timetabled.
  The lesson starts at 9.30 tomorrow instead of 10.30.
  They don't go back to school until next Monday.

Future continuous

Affirmative/Negative		
I / You / He / She / It / We / You / They	will	be flying this time next week.
I / You / He / She / It / We / You / They	won't	

Questions		
Will	I / you / he / she / it / we / you / they	be flying this time next week?

Short answers		
Yes,	I / you / he / she / it / we / you / they	will.
No,	I / you / he / she / it / we / you / they	won't.

- We form the **future continuous** with ***will/may/might*** + **be** + ***-ing***.
- We use the **future continuous** to talk about actions we believe will be in progress at a future time.
  In five years, he'll be living in Istanbul and working as a teacher.
  By 2025, everyone will be wearing smart watches.
- We can also use the **future continuous** to talk about future plans.
  I'll be leaving at 2 pm. I'm picking my little brother up from school, so I can't be late.
- We put question words at the beginning of a question.
  What will you be doing in 20 years' time?
  When will computers be cooking dinner for us?

Future perfect

Affirmative/Negative		
I / You / He / She / It / We / You / They	will have finished	the project by 2050.
I / You / He / She / It / We / You / They	won't have finished	

Questions			
Will	I / you / he / she / it / we / you / they	have finished	the project by 2050?

Short answers		
Yes,	I / you / he / she / it / we / you / they	will.
No,	I / you / he / she / it / we / you / they	won't.

- We form the **future perfect** with ***will*** + ***have*** + **past participle**.
- We use the **future perfect** for actions that will be completed before a certain time in the future.

LANGUAGE PRACTICE

Future tenses

1 Circle the correct options.

1 Mike's not sure yet, but he *'s going to* / *might* get a new bike.
2 Do you think it *'s going to* / *might* be a sunny day tomorrow?
3 Some scientists say the world's temperature *will* / *might* rise by four degrees in the next ten years.
4 Enjoy your holiday. I'm sure you *'ll* / *might* have a great time.
5 Tracy's mum *is going to* / *will* cook dinner.
6 I'm not feeling very well, so I *may not* / *won't* go to the match. I'll text you later.

2 Complete the sentences with the correct future form of the verbs in brackets.

1 This restaurant doesn't open (not open) until 5 pm this evening.
2 Do you think you ______ (pass) all your exams?
3 What time ______ (Tim / meet) us tomorrow?
4 I've decided I ______ (not buy) a new printer.
5 Larry hasn't decided yet, so he ______ (not have) dinner with us.
6 I ______ (order) pizza at the restaurant tonight.

3 Complete the conversations with the correct form of the verbs in the box.

buy need ~~overcook~~ start

1 A: Can I help you with dinner?
B: Yes. You fry the chicken because I 'll probably overcook it!
2 A: Where are you going?
B: Into town. I ______ a new coat.
3 A: What time do you want to meet?
B: The concert ______ at 8 pm, so let's say 7.30.
4 A: Is there enough food for everyone?
B: I don't know. I think we ______ some more bread.

Future continuous and future perfect

4 Complete the sentences with the future continuous form of the verbs in brackets.

1 What will you be doing (you / do) this time tomorrow?
2 My jeans are dirty, so I ______ (not wear) them tomorrow.
3 The music teacher says she ______ (not teach) us how to play this song.
4 While you're working hard, I ______ (enjoy) myself on holiday.
5 You can't meet him later, you ______ (write) your English essay.
6 Tomorrow's a national holiday, so we ______ (prepare) a special meal!

5 Complete the text with the future perfect form of the verbs in the box.

drink eat laugh see ~~sleep~~ spend

What do humans do in one year? By this time next year, you [1] will have slept for 2,372 hours and you [2] ______ over 1,000 hours on the Internet. You [3] ______ probably ______ some funny things, which means you [4] ______ for a total of 36.5 hours. If you're American, you [5] ______ around 46 slices of pizza and you [6] ______ probably ______ well over 800 litres of water.

6 Correct the mistake in each sentence.

1 This time tomorrow, ~~I'll have lying~~ on the beach in Italy. I'll be lying
2 In 20 years, we'll be built robots to do the cooking for us. ______
3 By the time tomorrow, I'll have finished all my exams. ______
4 I be not doing anything later, so call me. ______
5 Will have you started the dinner when I get home? ______
6 What will be you wearing to Chloe's party? ______

LANGUAGE REFERENCE

Deduction and possibility

- We often use ***can***, ***can't***, ***could***, ***may***, ***might*** and ***must*** + **infinitive** without *to* to say how possible or probable we think an action or event is.
  It can't be him! He never wears a hat to a party!
  She's late. She might be stuck in traffic.
  You must be tired after your long trip.
- We use ***can*** to make general statements about possibilities.
  They say that drinking too much coffee can be bad for you.
  Try drinking more water; it can help you feel more awake!
- We use ***can't*** to say that we think something is impossible or cannot be true.
  That can't be Samantha. She's in China!
  They can't be at home. I saw them leaving an hour ago.
- We use ***could***, ***may*** and ***might*** to say we think something is possible.
  You could have an infection; that's why you're feeling bad.
  A: Who's that man?
  B: I don't know. He may be her husband.
  It might be cold outside, so I'll take a coat.
- We use ***must*** when we think something is highly probable.
  She's not answering her phone. She must be busy.

Obligation, prohibition, necessity and advice

- We use ***must*** and ***have to*** to say that it is necessary to do something.
  Visitors must complete the form and then give it to the receptionist.
  We have to fill in this application and then send it to the office.
- We often use ***must*** when the obligation comes from the speaker – it's something the speaker considers important.
  You must do your homework before you go to Greg's house.
  I must get my grandfather a present for his birthday. I forgot last year!
- ***Must*** is followed by an infinitive without *to*.
- We use ***have to*** to say what it is necessary to do.
  You have to answer all the questions in the exam.
  He has to wear a uniform at school.
- We often use ***have to*** when we talk about laws or rules.
  You have to get good exam results to get in to this university.
  He's angry because he has to take his hat off in school.
- ***Have to*** is follow by an infinitive.
- We use ***don't have to*** to say that it is not necessary to do something, but that you can do it if you want.
  You don't have to help me with my experiment.
  She doesn't have to get up early tomorrow.
- Question words go at the beginning of the question.
  How much homework do you have to do every day?
  When do we have to make a decision?
- We use ***had to*** to say that it was necessary to do something in the past.
  I had to leave school early as I wasn't feeling well.
- We use ***can't*** and ***mustn't*** to say something is prohibited by law or rules.
  I can't take my new phone to school – it's the rule.
  You mustn't use your calculator in the exam.
- We use ***need to*** to express necessity in the present. We use ***don't need to*** to show a lack of necessity.
  I need to get home before my parents get angry.
  They don't need to leave now. It's still early.
- We use ***should('nt)*** and ***ought to*** to give advice. ***Should('nt)*** and ***ought to*** both mean 'I think it's (not) a good idea for someone to do this.'
  You should take the bus. It will be faster.
  They shouldn't eat that. They're going to get sick.
  We ought to pay attention. This might be in the exam.

LANGUAGE PRACTICE

UNIT 4

Deduction and possibility

1 Circle the correct options.

1 I'm not sure, but I think this gold (*may not*) / *can't* be real.
2 Reading in bed at night *can* / *must* help you fall asleep quicker.
3 I don't know what's in the box. It *could* / *can* be a present.
4 Harry failed two exams. He *couldn't* / *can't* be very happy.
5 Have a drink of water. You *might* / *must* be very thirsty after the match.
6 The doctor's not very sure. She says it *might* / *must* be serious.

2 Use the prompts to write the second sentence.

1 I haven't eaten all day. You / be hungry
You must be very hungry.
2 It's eleven o'clock at night. Freya / be in bed
______
3 I feel sick. You / need to sit down
______
4 That boy looks like Freddie, but Freddie's in Turkey. That / be Freddie
______
5 Max got up late. He / not arrive on time for his first class
______
6 That cheese is three weeks old! It / be very smelly
______

Obligation, prohibition, necessity and advice

3 Are the sentences about obligation (O), prohibition (P), necessity (N) or advice (A)?

1 You mustn't use your mobile phone in class. P
2 I probably don't need to wear a coat today. ___
3 I think Lauren should study engineering. ___
4 You ought to try switching the computer off. ___
5 You must write at least 100 words. ___
6 What do I have to do to be successful? ___

4 Complete the email with the phrases in the box.

don't have to worry	~~don't need to bring~~
have to take	mustn't forget
need to pack	ought to buy

Hi Ethan

I'm so glad you're coming to visit us. It's really warm here, so you [1] don't need to bring a coat. However, you [2] ______ your swimming trunks because we're going to the beach. We'll [3] ______ the train, so I [4] ______ our tickets tomorrow. You [5] ______ about bringing a towel because we've got loads, but you [6] ______ your sun cream!!

See you on Friday!

5 Complete the second sentence so that it means the same as the first. Use no more than three words.

1 Don't shout. I can hear everything you're saying.
You don't need to shout because I can hear everything you say.
2 It's not a very good idea to call him now.
You probably ______ him now.
3 I had an appointment with the doctor yesterday.
I ______ and see the doctor yesterday.
4 There's no need to worry about making lunch.
You ______ to worry about making lunch.
5 No running in the corridors.
Students ______ in the corridors.
6 That car must be very expensive.
That car ______ cheap.

LANGUAGE BANK

STARTER

Vocabulary

Travel

accommodation backpacking holiday resort
sightseeing tourist attraction trip

Music and theatre

audience lines part
rehearsal scene show

Ways of communicating

describe greet post
shake hands shout smile
translate wave whisper

Language in action

Present and past simple and continuous
Present perfect and past simple

Writing

Useful language

Starting and ending an informal email

Hello … Hi …
How are you? / Thanks for your email. / How are things?
I'm writing to … / I just wanted to say …
See you soon. / Bye for now. / Write back soon.
Take care, … / Love …

UNIT 1

Vocabulary

Describing clothes and shoes

baggy checked cotton denim flat
flowery high-heeled long-sleeved
plain spotted striped tight

Verbs for clothes and shoes

do up fit fold go out of fashion
go with hang up match
suit undo wear out

Language in action

Present perfect simple and present perfect continuous
Modifiers

Speaking

Everyday English

check out
fashion victim
in
out there

Useful language

I don't know if …
I'm not a huge fan of …
I think maybe …
That's … er … different!
They're not exactly my style.

Writing

Useful language

Great post!
I had no idea that …
It got me thinking about …
I've decided to …
Since reading your post I've …
Thanks for sharing!

LANGUAGE BANK

UNIT 2

Vocabulary

Phrasal verbs: changes

do without end up go back go through
look forward to move out move to
settle down sign up try out
turn down turn out

Parts of objects

button cable cover display handle
key lens lid plug strap

Language in action

used to, *would* and past simple
Past perfect with *never*, *already*, *by* (*then*), *by the time*

Speaking

Everyday English

all over again
I'm not surprised.
old-school
That's it.

Useful language

Is it some kind of … ?
I've messed it up.
Like this, you mean?
What you do is, you …
You'll have to …

Writing

Useful language

firstly
in addition
in conclusion
secondly
therefore
this means that

UNIT 3

Vocabulary

Cooking verbs

bake chop fry grate grill
heat overcook peel roast
season slice spread

Quantities

a chunk of a cup of a handful of a packet of
a piece of a pinch of a slice of
a splash of a spoonful of a sprinkle of

Language in action

Present tense and *be going* to for future plans and intentions
Predictions with *be going to*, *will* and *may*/*might*
Future continuous and future perfect

Speaking

Everyday English

a fair amount
ages
a piece of cake
Is that it?
yummy

Useful language

Don't forget to … (+ verb)
Once that's done …
Start by … (+ *-ing*)
While that's … (+ *-ing*)
You'll need …

Writing

Useful language

… is here to stay
… isn't going anywhere
Watch this space
What could be tastier than … ?
… will be around forever
… will be the norm

LANGUAGE BANK

UNIT 4

Vocabulary

The five senses

feel feel like look look like
smell smell like sound
sound like taste taste like touch

Describing texture, sound, taste, etc.

colourful faint rough sharp shiny
smelly smooth sour spicy transparent

Language in action

Modals of deduction and possibility
Obligation, prohibition, necessity and advice

Speaking

Everyday English

Bingo!
I give up!
I guess so.
nice and warm/hot, etc.
Sure, why not?

Useful language

Guess again.
Guess what it is / they are.
I guess they must be …
Perhaps it's something (+ adjective)
They're definitely some kind of …

Writing

Useful language

According to …
At the age of …
including …
… is known as …
… was born on … and grew up in.

UNIT 5

Vocabulary

Processes

attract collect communicate connect
create deliver develop measure
produce solve supply waste

Extreme adjectives

boiling deafening dreadful enormous
fascinating freezing gorgeous
marvellous stunning terrifying

Language in action

The passive
Question tags and questions with prepositions

Speaking

Everyday English

… and everything
Er, not exactly.
I'd say it was …
Oh, man
Wanna … ?

Useful language

Are you kidding me?
I can't believe you actually …
I find that hard to believe.
Seriously?
You can't be serious.

Writing

Useful language

… deserves to win because …
I'm absolutely certain that …
The highlight of a visit to … is …
the … that impressed me the most was …
Without a doubt …

LANGUAGE BANK

UNIT 6

Vocabulary

Verb collocations with get, take and have

get a lot out of   get bored   get lost
get on my nerves   get to know
have doubts   have fun   have the chance
take advantage of   take an interest in
take pleasure in   take risks

Inspiration and challenge

Nouns	**Verbs**
bravery	achieve
challenge	encourage
determination	inspire
obstacle	overcome
opportunity	support

Language in action

First and second conditional
Third conditional

Speaking

Everyday English

Come on!
Good for you!
not really
seriously
You've got to be joking!

Useful language

Encouraging

Don't worry, you'll be fine.
You can do it!
You'll feel really proud afterwards.
You'll never know unless you try.

Responding

That's easy for you to say.
What if … (+ past simple)?

Writing

Useful language

For example … / For instance … / such as …
Furthermore … / On the one hand …
I personally believe (that) …
On the other hand …
In conclusion …

UNIT 7

Vocabulary

Feelings

amused   annoyed   down   eager   glad
grateful   hopeful   hurt   insecure
peaceful   ridiculous   satisfied   thrilled

Expressions with heart and mind

be in two minds   bear in mind
break someone's heart   change your mind
close to your heart   cross your mind
have something on your mind   learn by heart
make your mind up
put your heart into something

Language in action

Gerunds and infinitives
Subject and object questions

Speaking

Everyday English

a little harsh
Don't mention it.
I swear
stressed out
That's kind of you …

Useful language

I can imagine.
Is there anything I can do to help?
It'll all be OK, you'll see.
That's not very nice.
What's the matter?

Writing

Useful language

It might be better (not) to …
It would definitely help to …
I would recommend … (+ *-ing*)
Whatever you do, don't …
Why don't you suggest … (+ *-ing*)?

LANGUAGE BANK

UNIT 8

Vocabulary

Advertising

ad blocker advert advertise brand buyer influence logo marketing company product review seller slogan

Internet verbs

build up comment on delete follow post shut down subscribe to switch off switch on vlog

Language in action

Defining and non-defining relative clauses
Indefinite, reflexive and reciprocal pronouns

Speaking

Everyday English

handy
I don't have a clue.
no-brainer
What's up?

Useful language

I can't recommend it/them enough!
I don't know where to start!
Is it easy to use?
It's the best thing …
(It) would be ideal for …
You really ought to …

Writing

Useful language

… is included.
It allows you to …
It is designed to be used …
One of its best features is …
The one thing that's missing is …

UNIT 9

Vocabulary

Reporting verbs

admit announce apologise claim complain confirm deny discover insist promise refuse suggest

Adverbs of time and manner

after a while eventually fluently gradually nowadays occasionally patiently regularly secretly surprisingly

Language in action

Reported statements and commands
Reported questions

Speaking

Everyday English

Hey!
Let me guess.
show-off
sort of
to make matters worse

Useful language

Basically, what happened was …
It was so (+ adjective)
So anyway, …
The next thing I knew …
You'll never guess what happened …

Writing

Useful language

An email

A man/woman from …
He/She announced/explained/admitted that …
'…,' he/she said
Surprisingly/Nowadays etc. …
When asked … he/she answered/explained/said …

IRREGULAR VERBS

Infinitive	Past simple	Past participle
be	was/were	been
beat	beat	beaten
become	became	become
begin	began	begun
bite	bit	bitten
blow	blew	blown
break	broke	broken
bring	brought	brought
build	built	built
buy	bought	bought
catch	caught	caught
choose	chose	chosen
come	came	come
cost	cost	cost
cut	cut	cut
do	did	done
draw	drew	drawn
drink	drank	drunk
drive	drove	driven
eat	ate	eaten
fall	fell	fallen
feel	felt	felt
fight	fought	fought
find	found	found
fly	flew	flown
forget	forgot	forgotten
get	got	got
give	gave	given
go	went	gone
grow	grew	grown
hang	hung	hung
have	had	had
hear	heard	heard
hide	hid	hidden
hit	hit	hit
hold	held	held
hurt	hurt	hurt
keep	kept	kept
know	knew	known
leave	left	left
lend	lent	lent

Infinitive	Past simple	Past participle
let	let	let
lie	lied	lied
light	lit	lit
lose	lost	lost
make	made	made
mean	meant	meant
meet	met	met
pay	paid	paid
put	put	put
read	read	read
ride	rode	ridden
ring	rang	rung
rise	rose	risen
run	ran	run
say	said	said
see	saw	seen
sell	sold	sold
send	sent	sent
shine	shone	shone
shoot	shot	shot
show	showed	shown
shut	shut	shut
sing	sang	sung
sit	sat	sat
sleep	slept	slept
speak	spoke	spoken
spend	spent	spent
stand	stood	stood
steal	stole	stolen
swim	swam	swum
take	took	taken
teach	taught	taught
tear	tore	torn
tell	told	told
think	thought	thought
throw	threw	thrown
understand	understood	understood
wake	woke	woken
wear	wore	worn
win	won	won
write	wrote	written

Student's Book acknowledgements

The authors and publishers acknowledge the following sources of copyright material and are grateful for the permissions granted. While every effort has been made, it has not always been possible to identify the sources of all the material used, or to trace all copyright holders. If any omissions are brought to our notice, we will be happy to include the appropriate acknowledgements on reprinting & in the next update to the digital edition, as applicable.

Key: CLIL = Content and Language Integrated Learning; EM: End Matter, SU = Starter Unit; U = Unit, VB = Vocabulary Bank.

Text

U01: Text about Moziah Bridge. Copyrighyt © Adriann Ranta Zurhellen. Reproduced with permission; **U04**: Text about Neil Harbisson. Copyright © Neil Harbisson. Reproduced with kind permission; Text about surfer Bethany Hamilton. Copyright © Becky Hamilton. Reproduced with kind permission.

Photography

The following photographs are sourced from Getty Images.

SU: Dave and Les Jacobs/Blend Images; Django/E+; jhorrocks/E+; Vostok/Moment; Lennart Schreiber/EyeEm; Adie Bush/Cultura; Hill Street Studios/Blend Images; vetdoctor/iStock/Getty Images Plus; yayayoyo/iStock/Getty Images Plus; Tigatelu/iStock/Getty Images Plus Elizabeth Parsons/EyeEm Premium John Lawson, Belhaven/Moment Open Yavuz Meyveci/iStock Editorial/Getty Images Plus; arabianEye arabianEye; **U1:** DigiPub/Moment Open; Henrik Sorensen/Stone; Halfpoint/iStock/Getty Images Plus; Halfpoint/iStock/Getty Images Plus; Timur Emek/Getty Images Entertainment; Maciej Frolow/The Image Bank; Artur Debat/Moment Mobile; Sidekick/E+; Pascal Deloche/Godong/Corbis Documentary; Chris Ryan/OJO Images; Andy Crawford/Dorling Kindersley; khvost/iStock/Getty Images Plus; GeorgePeters/E+; Paul Simcock; Erik Isakson; Feifei Cui-Paoluzzo/Moment; Hans-Peter Merten/The Image Bank; jboater/iStock/Getty Images Plus; PeterHermesFurian/iStock/Getty Images Plus; Rohappy/iStock/Getty Images Plus; Leon Bennett/WireImage; ozgurdonmaz/iStock/Getty Images Plus; mocoo/iStock/Getty Images Plus; **U2:** Jennifer Perry/EyeEm; mantaphoto/E+; Mark Daffey/Lonely Planet Images; KIKILOMBO/iStock/Getty Images Plus; alejandrophotography/iStock/Getty Images Plus; Emanuele Ravecca/EyeEm; Science Photo Library; luoman/E+; Spod/iStock/Getty Images Plus; Steve Shott/Dorling Kindersley; Gregory_DUBUS/iStock/Getty Images Plus; DNY59/E+; Oleg Golovnev/EyeEm; Westend61; Betsie Van der Meer/Stone; ajr_images/iStock/Getty Images Plus; pixdeluxe/iStock/Getty Images Plus; LisaAFischer/iStock/Getty Images Plus; H. Armstrong Roberts/ClassicStock/Archive Photos; Allan Tannenbaum/Archive Photos; Michael Ochs Archives; funky-data/E+; cjmacer/iStock Editorial/Getty Images Plus; mocoo/iStock/Getty Images Plus; **U3:** WIN-Initiative; tgasser/iStock/Getty Images Plus; BravissimoS/iStock/Getty Images Plus; EasterBunnyUK/iStock/Getty Images Plus; Valentyn Semenov/EyeEm; DonNichols/iStock/Getty Images Plus; mikroman6/Moment; Eskay Lim/EyeEm; Jamie Grill/The Image Bank; Bill Oxford/E+; Capelle.r/Moment; Jamie Stamey/iStock/Getty Images Plus; Ian Cuming/Ikon Images; NosUA/iStock/Getty Images Plus; D-Keine/E+; Andrey Suslov/iStock/Getty Images Plus; Sirikunkrittaphuk/iStock/Getty Images Plus; Creativ Studio Heinemann; Slawomir Tomas/EyeEm; Maximilian Stock Ltd./Photographer's Choice; Hayley Harrison/The Image Bank; Dorling Kindersley; GorynVD/iStock/Getty Images Plus; William Whitehurst/Corbis; Blend Images - KidStock/Brand X Pictures; KidStock/Blend Images; Maica/iStock/Getty Images Plus; Diana Miller/Cultura; Peter Cade/The Image Bank; marilyna/iStock/Getty Images Plus; Tetra Images; Tobias Titz; Hauke Dressler/LOOK-foto/LOOK; Neydtstock/iStock/Getty Images Plus; Melanitta/iStock/Getty Images Plus; Jami Tarris/Corbis Documentary; GMVozd/E+; Image Source; Tanya Zouev/StockFood Creative; Neustockimages/iStock/Getty Images Plus; Tim Platt/The Image Bank; Westend61; Rasulovs/iStock/Getty Images Plus; WoodyUpstate/iStock/Getty Images Plus; vovashevchuk/iStock/Getty Images Plus; Joff Lee/Photolibrary; Rosemary Calvert/Photographer's Choice; petekarici/E+; Jbryson/iStock/Getty Images Plus; mocoo/iStock/Getty Images Plus; **U4:** Buena Vista Images/DigitalVision; Alberto Ghizzi Panizza/Biosphoto; Arrow/DigitalVision; manoa/Moment; Paula Daniëlse/Moment Open; Tony Robins/Photolibrary; Andy Sotiriou/Photodisc; Tai/Moment; Raimund Linke/Oxford Scientific; bugphai/iStock/Getty Images Plus; Jamie Brand/EyeEm; Ian O'Leary/Dorling Kindersley; Sam Edwards; Danita Delimont/Gallo Images; Jutta Klee/Canopy; Jacqui Hurst/Photolibrary; hphimagelibrary/Gallo Images; Foodcollection; Christian Adams/Photographer's Choice; Coleman515/iStock/Getty Images Plus; DragonImages/iStock/Getty Images Plus; bergamont/iStock/Getty Images Plus; Stephen Stickler/Photographer's Choice; Kirshal/iStock/Getty Images Plus Douglas Sacha/Moment; Natthakan Jommanee/EyeEm; kiankhoon/iStock/Getty Images Plus; c11yg/iStock/Getty Images Plus; Bruce Mclean/EyeEm; AVIcons/iStock/Getty Images Plus; Amin Yusifov/iStock/Getty Images Plus; mocoo/iStock/Getty Images Plus; **FF1**: Anthony Lee/OJO Images; vgajic/E+; Rafael Ben-Ari/The Image Bank; Imgorthand/E+; **VBS**: Asia-Pacific Images Studio/iStock/Getty Images Plus; Watchara Panyajun/EyeEm; majaiva/E+; Caiaimage/Sam Edwards; LeoPatrizi/E+; Brian Feinzimer/Getty Images Entertainment; **VB1**: domin_domin/iStock/Getty Images Plus; Ng Sok Lian/EyeEm; kitthanes/iStock/Getty Images Plus; Floortje/E+; olga_sweet/iStock/Getty Images Plus; Lalouetto/iStock/Getty Images Plus; Mehmet Hilmi Barcin/E+; FlamingPumpkin/iStock/Getty Images Plus; mawielobob/iStock/Getty Images Plus; Tarzhanova/iStock/Getty Images Plus; **VB2**: Karl Tapales/Moment; Melanie Hobson/EyeEm; kk2s/iStock/Getty Images Plus; MartinPrescott/E+; Gado Images/Photodisc; TARIK KIZILKAYA/E+; Jorge Alberto Bohorquez Suarez/EyeEm; LeMusique/iStock/Getty Images Plus; JohnGollop/E+; JuergenBosse/iStock/Getty Images Plus; **VB3**: tirc83/iStock/Getty Images Plus; KucherAV/iStock/Getty Images Plus; dlewis33/E+; Lucy Lambriex/DigitalVision; Adam Radosavljevic/EyeEm; Claire Gunn; lolostock/iStock/Getty Images Plus; uuurska/iStock/Getty Images Plus; Lakshmi3/iStock/Getty Images Plus; Westend61; Yurikr/iStock/Getty Images Plus; Paula/FOAP; **VB4**: Dalia Rady/EyeEm; DragonFly/iStock/Getty Images Plus; Pierre-Yves Babelon/Antananarivo, Antananarivo Province, Madagascar; Mike Whitby/EyeEm; DAJ; Cody Duncan; Stefka Pavlova/Moment; Theerapan Bhumirat/EyeEm; luknaja/iStock/Getty Images Plus; Rachan Panya/EyeEm; **CLIL2** : Bettmann; **CLIL4:** VICTOR HABBICK VISIONS/SCIENCE PHOTO LIBRARY.

The following photographs are sourced from other sources.

U4: courtesy of Peter Cernik MA; Copyright © Neil Harbisson. Reproduced with kind permission; **ICONS:** Prithvi/Noun Project; Agni/Noun Project; mikicon/Noun Project; Baboon designs, US/Noun Project; Tanguy Keryhuel, FR/Noun Project; Icons Bazaar/Noun Project; Adrien Coquet, FR/Noun Project; Vectors Market/Noun Project; TukTuk Design/Noun Project; iconsphere, ID/Noun Project; i cons, US/Noun Project; kim Eriksson/Noun Project; Lloyd Humphreys, DK/Noun Project; Delwar Hossain, BD/Noun Project; Kirby Wu, TW/Noun Project; Magicon, HU/Noun Project; Baboon designs, US/Noun Project.

Illustrations

SU: Sean Longcroft; **U2, EM:** Claire Rollet (Illustration Web); **U2, U4:** Joanna Kerr.

Video Stills

The following stills are sourced from Getty Images.

U1: Bronek Kaminski/one80: Signature; Merlas/iStock/Getty Images Plus; FG Trade/Creatas Video; Merlas/iStock/Getty Images Plus; **U2:** RWP UK/DigitalVision; Sirinarth Mekvorawuth/EyeEm; taavet/Creatas Video+/Getty Images Plus; **U3:** Neustockimages/Creatas Video+/Getty Images Plus; Multi-bits/Image Bank Film; Besjunior/iStock/Getty Images Plus; andresr/Creatas Video; **U4:** nattanan726/Creatas Video+/Getty Images Plus; gpointstudio/Creatas Video+/Getty Images Plus; yacobchuk/iStock/Getty Images Plus.

The following stills are sourced from other source.

SU–U4: Lucentum Digital.

Cover design and illustrations: Collaborate Agency.

Video produced by Lucentum Digital.

Audio produced by Creative Listening.

Typeset by Blooberry Design.

Workbook acknowledgements

The authors and publishers acknowledge the following sources of copyright material and are grateful for the permissions granted. While every effort has been made, it has not always been possible to identify the sources of all the material used, or to trace all copyright holders. If any omissions are brought to our notice, we will be happy to include the appropriate acknowledgements on reprinting & in the next update to the digital edition, as applicable.

Key: SU = Starter Unit, **U** = Unit, **VE** = Vocabulary Extra.

Photography

The following photographs are sourced from Getty Images.

SU: Harald Nachtmann/Moment; Anestis Karagiannopoulos/EyeEm; Matteo Colombo/DigitalVision; oleksii arseniuk/iStock/Getty Images Plus; Anastasiia_M/iStock/Getty Images Plus; chokkicx/DigitalVision Vectors; platongkoh/iStock/Getty Images Plus; Hans Neleman/The Image Bank; Hemera Technologies/PhotoObjects.net/Getty Images Plus; Steve Debenport/E+; John Cancalosi/Photolibrary; Hill Street Studios/DigitalVision; **U1**: PeopleImages/E+; Pawel Libera/Photolibrary; JackF/iStock/Getty Images Plus; Chiyacat/iStock/Getty Images Plus; rolfbodmer/E+; Jitalia17/E+; component2/iStock/Getty Images Plus; **U2**: Julie Moquet/EyeEm; Ariel Skelley/DigitalVision; JRL/The Image Bank; Don Mason; Aaron Black/Aurora; Image Source/Image Source; Ljupco/iStock/Getty Images Plus; akova/iStock/Getty Images Plus; hh5800/iStock/Getty Images Plus; homydesign/iStock/Getty Images Plus; Bet_Noire/iStock/Getty Images Plus; Valerie Loiseleux/iStock/Getty Images Plus; Whiteway/iStock/Getty Images Plus; Vasily Pindyurin Caiaimage/Sam Edwards/Caiaimage; Debrocke/ClassicStock/Archive Photos; kertlis/E+; Creativ Studio Heinemann; Wan Muhammad Faisalludin Wan Azeland/EyeEm; Peter Dazeley/Photographer's Choice; PhotoAlto/Laurence Mouton/PhotoAlto Agency RF Collections; Richard Newstead/Moment; Oliver Cleve/Photographer's Choice; TommL/E+; Nick Wright/Photolibrary; ET-ARTWORKS/DigitalVision Vectors; NiseriN/iStock/Getty Images Plus; **U3**: Dave King/Dorling Kindersley; Guillermo Murcia/Moment Open; Jody Louie took this picture/Moment; Joy Skipper/Photolibrary; Giles Clarke/Contributor/Getty Images Europe; Rosemary Calvert/Photographer's Choice; alantobey/E+; Gavin Hellier/robertharding/robertharding; Anne Ackermann/DigitalVision; George Mdivanian/EyeEm; erierika/iStock/Getty Images Plus; GOSPHOTODESIGN/StockFood Creative; Simon McGill/Moment; Chris Everard/The Image Bank; anna1311/iStock/Getty Images Plus; Christian Vierig/Contributor/Getty Images Entertainment; Evgeniyaphotography/iStock/Getty Images Plus; imaginima/iStock/Getty Images Plus; H. Armstrong Roberts/ClassicStock/Archive Photos; Highwaystarz-Photography/iStock/Getty Images Plus; **U4**: Elizaveta Pahomova/EyeEm; kiszon pascal/Moment; Guillaume CHANSON/Moment; Kristina Strasunske/Moment; Sam Edwards/Caiaimage; Johann van Heerden/Moment Open; Nenov/Moment Open; Ed Freeman//Stone; Sally Anscombe/DigitalVision; Henrik Sorensen/DigitalVision; Glynne Joseph Pritchard/Contributor/Moment Mobile; Noam Galai/Contributor/Getty Images Entertainment; Tony Barson/Contributor/FilmMagic; Fuse/Corbis; Danita Delimont/Gallo Images; Kevin Winter/Staff/Getty Images Entertainment; RusticFOTO/iStock/Getty Images Plus; Eerik/iStock/Getty Images Plus.

Illustrations

U1: Claire Rollet; **U3:** Joanna Kerr; **U4:** Howarth from The Big Red illustration; **VE**: Howarth from The Big Red illustration Agency; Joanna Kerr.

Typesetting: Blooberry Design

Cover design and illustrations: Collaborate Agency

Video production: Lucentum Digital

Audio recordings: Creative Listening

Freelance editing: Matthew Duffy, Jacqueline French and Jacqueline Walkden.